LIFT YOUR MOOD NOW

SIMPLE THINGS YOU CAN DO
TO BEAT THE BLUES

JOHN D. PRESTON, PSY.D.

NEW HARBINGER PUBLICATIONS, INC.

Distributed in the U.S.A. by Publishers Group West; in Canada by Raincoast Books; in Great Britain by Airlift Book Company, Ltd.; in South Africa by Real Books, Ltd.; in Australia by Boobook; and in New Zealand by Tandem Press.

Copyright © 2001 by John Preston
        New Harbinger Publications, Inc.
        5674 Shattuck Avenue
        Oakland, CA 94609

Cover design by Poulson/Gluck Designs
Edited by Carole Honeychurch
Book design by Michele Waters

ISBN 1-57224-243-4 Paperback

New Harbinger Publications' Web site address: www.newharbinger.com

03   02   01

10   9   8   7   6   5   4   3   2   1

First printing

To my good friends: Frank Mahoney and Jan Groesz

Contents

Part Two
Stabilizing Your Brain and Biology

Part Four
Combating Low Self-Esteem

Part Five
Understanding and Managing Intense Emotions

Part Six
Staying Connected and Avoiding Relapse

Acknowledgments

I would like to gratefully acknowledge the following people: my editors Carole Honeychurch and Angela Watrous, for your excellent suggestions and guidance; Dr. Matt McKay, for your ongoing support and encouragement; and Michelle Housh—superb, as usual!

To John P. McGinis and his colleagues with Senior Peer Counseling, many thanks for your invaluable service to our community.

To Dr. Mary M. Maaga, thanks for all you have shared and the positive impact you have had on the lives of so many.

A special heartfelt thanks to my clients during the past twenty-five years, for all you have taught me about healing and emotional growth.

And, as always, to Bonnie, my best friend and soulmate; thanks for everything (and I mean everything!).

J.P.

Part One

First Things First

"The best way out is through."

—Robert Frost

Depression grabs people. It's stubborn, persistent, and relentless. Most people who experience depression attempt to "snap out of it," ignore it, or at least endure it. But the nature of depression is to invade your life; it can rob you of vitality and demolish hope. No one has ever defeated depression simply by gritting their teeth or engaging in a "cheer yourself up" version of denial. One way or another, you will be moving through depression, but there clearly are ways to go about this that can reduce suffering and promote recovery.

What works to combat depression are professional treatment and action-oriented self-help approaches. That's what this book is about. You are going to learn very specific action plans for helping yourself and you can begin *right now*.

The starting point is understanding something about what you are up against, and we will take a quick look at what depression is in the first chapter of part 1. Then we'll move directly into the first steps you can take to tackle depression head-on and begin to regain your life.

Chapter One

Understanding Depression and Taking Action

"Into each heart . . . some tears must fall"
—Whitfield and Holland

Everyone has a down day once in a while; everyone has the blues now and then. Woven into the fabric of life are inevitable disappointments, failures, and setbacks. And, sooner or later, each of us will experience very painful losses when friends or loved ones die. Unfortunately this is a part of the price of membership in the human race.

Beyond these common emotional elements of life is the experience of clinical depression. One out of five of us will experience this. Given this extraordinarily high prevalence rate, it's hard to imagine that any family in our country can escape having at least one family member or close friend suffer from depression.

There are fundamental differences between mild or temporary encounters with despair or sadness and clinical depression (also often referred to as "major depression" or "unipolar depression"). Likewise, there are significant differences between normal grief and clinical depression. At first glance, these human experiences may seem similar, but upon closer inspection, the differences are clear.

Clinical depression is not just a feeling. It always is a cluster of symptoms, including, but not limited to, the following:

- Mood changes (sadness, intense irritability, feeling easily frustrated)

- Low self-esteem, feelings of worthlessness, lack of self-confidence

- Extremely negative thinking, including pessimism, a bleak view of the future, thoughts of hopelessness, thoughts about suicide, brooding, worrying, fretting

- A loss of interest in most life activities; a profound lack of vitality

- Marked changes in physical functioning including: sleep disturbances, fatigue and low energy, loss of sex drive, and changes in appetite and weight

Clinical depression lasts a long time. Most people who are depressed have done their best to "snap out of it," only to quickly notice that they are pulled back again into depression. The typical bout of major depression, if not treated, will last from nine to fifteen months. After this prolonged time of suffering, about 75 percent of people will gradually come out of the depression; for the other 25 percent, it can hang on for months or years.

Fortunately, with appropriate treatment, most people respond and recover.

Treatment Is Essential!

In the United States it is estimated that two-thirds of people suffering with clinical depression *never* receive treatment. This is especially disturbing since most depressions can be very successfully treated. Left untreated, people suffer tremendously and needlessly. Lives are ruined, marriages fall apart, school performance plummets, jobs are lost, health can become compromised, many turn to increased alcohol use/abuse, and some people commit suicide.

This need not happen. The keys to avoiding these results are:

- Taking action to get professional help, which includes psychotherapy and perhaps treatment with antidepressant medications.

- Learning about depression and making sure that family members learn about it as well. During recovery from depression, ongoing support from family members can be crucial, but for this to occur, they must become well informed about depression.

- Developing an attitude of compassion for yourself is critical. Stem the tide of harsh self-criticism, and be decent to yourself.

- Finally (and this takes us to the purpose of this book), what can be of tremendous help while combating depression is to adopt an action-oriented strategy that pulls out all of the stops, using a number of self-help approaches that have been shown to be powerful approaches to reducing depression. These approaches are outlined in this book and are presented in a straightforward and easily understandable format. Combined with appropriate professional treatment, such techniques can help speed up the process of recovery.

So, let's get started.

Chapter Two

How to Use
This Book

"Depression feels hopeless even though the prognosis is excellent."
—David Burns, M.D.

"But I don't have the energy or motivation to read a book!" If you find yourself thinking this, you are not alone. Depression saps energy, it interferes with the ability to concentrate, and many, if not most times, a big part of depression is feeling pessimistic ("It won't help me") or not very motivated ("Well, maybe it helps others, but I don't feel motivated to do anything about it"). Often the prospect of reading a book or following through with exercises just seems overwhelming when you're depressed. I know this, and this is the main reason for a book like this. What follows are chapters that can easily be read in about five minutes or less, and techniques that are easy to implement.

In each chapter you'll be learning action strategies that have solid research support for their effectiveness. This book and the various strategies have been designed to be used either solely as self-help or in combination with psychotherapy. Many of the leading experts on the treatment of depression agree that self-help exercise or other types of therapy "homework" can significantly speed up the time it takes to recover from depression and may also help to prevent a relapse or recurrence of depression. And an all-out assault on depression (i.e., professional treatment and the use of multiple self-help strategies) has the greatest chance of resolving depression quickly.

Let me suggest the following. Please at least read the next two chapters (it will take about ten minutes) and see how it goes. Then scan the titles of the other chapters. See which ones fit problems that you personally are experiencing. Each day read one or two chapters. Each one will take about five minutes to read.

If you find it very difficult or impossible to read or to try out the exercises, please do not give up. This is not at all unusual. Many people need to have some professional help first, and after a few weeks, most people do begin to feel less depressed. Then it may be possible to come back to this book.

Each year several *million* people in our country successfully recover from depression. Please keep in mind, beliefs like "I'll never get over this depression" are manifestations of the disorder (when you're depressed, your thinking is almost always negative and pessimistic). With depression, there are no quick fixes. What is possible and does occur for the majority of depressed people in treatment is that, within a few weeks, the depression begins to loosen its hold, and after a few more weeks, it often subsides and life begins to return to normal.

Take action now. I'm glad you bought this book; I think it will help.

Is Professional Help Necessary?

When depression is serious, professional treatment (psychotherapy and possibly antidepressant medication treatment) is necessary. However, in milder cases, family support and self-help approaches may be all that is required.

Before starting with this program of self-help, please check the following list. If any of the following are true for you, then strongly consider seeing a mental health professional:

- The depression is seriously interfering with work, school, or significant personal relationships.

- There are marked changes in physical/biological functions, such as frequently disturbed sleep, severe exhaustion and fatigue, or noticeable changes in appetite, weight, or sex drive.

- Alcohol or drug use has been escalating or is hard to control.

- You have been experiencing serious thoughts about self-harm or suicide.

- Self-help approaches, if pursued for more than one month, fail to result in noticeable improvements in depressive symptoms.

Locate a therapist by asking your doctor for a referral or by contacting your local Mental Health Association (most can help people find a therapist). It's important to find a therapist who has specific training and experience in treating depression. Don't be bashful about making phone calls to inquire about a therapist's areas of expertise. You will be deciding about hiring this person as your mental health consultant and you have a perfect right to make sure you are seeing the appropriate person.

Lots of depressed people put off seeking professional help. Often months and months can pass as the person tries to maintain hope that the depression will fade away on its own. If you believe that you need professional help, *take action now*.

So, let's get started. The next chapter will talk about the first steps to take so that in the next few minutes you can begin to overcome depression.

Chapter Three

Getting Started and Tracking Your Recovery

Psychologists have found that the on-going recording of depressive symptoms actually helps to decrease depression. How can this be possible?

As people begin to engage in either professional treatment or self-help for depression it's not unusual, within a week or so, to see some symptoms begin to subside. Yet when asked if they are feeling better (during the first two or three weeks of treatment) most depressed people say, "I'm no better." Why can't they see their improvement? The answer is that one symptom of depression that takes somewhat longer to resolve is *negative thinking*. Depressed individuals have a strong tendency to ignore early signs of improvement and focus more exclusively on ongoing negative, sad, or pessimistic thoughts and feelings.

I'd like to *strongly* encourage you to complete the following depression rating scale now and once a week thereafter, and periodically look back to the original rating and compare. (Please make extra copies of the rating scale.)

This approach can help you carefully evaluate and track your recovery. Week to week, the rating scale is kind of like a thermometer measuring the intensity and frequency of your symptoms. When changes begin to take place, and are noted on particular items of the rating scale, you can see your progress clearly. Often, this evidence that you're getting better can make you start to feel more hopeful. Realistic and accurate tracking of improvement helps to foster and maintain hope.

Weekly Depression Rating Scale

Please read each item below and determine which statement is true for you. Then, place an "**X**" in the appropriate box to indicate how often you feel the statement applies to you **during the past week**. Be sure to rate every item.

Example	None or a little of the time	Some of the time	Most or all of the time
1. *I feel sad*		X	

During the Past Week	None or a little of the time	Some of the time*	Most or all of the time**
1. Wake up at night or in the early morning, unable to return to sleep			
2. Very restless sleep			
3. Loss of energy, fatigued			
4. Decreased sex drive			
5. Unable to enjoy life; have lost a zest for life			
6. Have withdrawn from others			
7. Strong thoughts about suicide			
8. Loss of appetite			
9. Memory problem, forgetfulness, poor concentration			
10. Feel irritable or easily frustrated			
11. Feelings of sadness, hopelessness, or unhappiness			
12. Sleeping a lot			
13. Feelings of low self-esteem			
14. Apathy or low motivation			

*   3—5 days of the last week

**   6—7 days of the last week

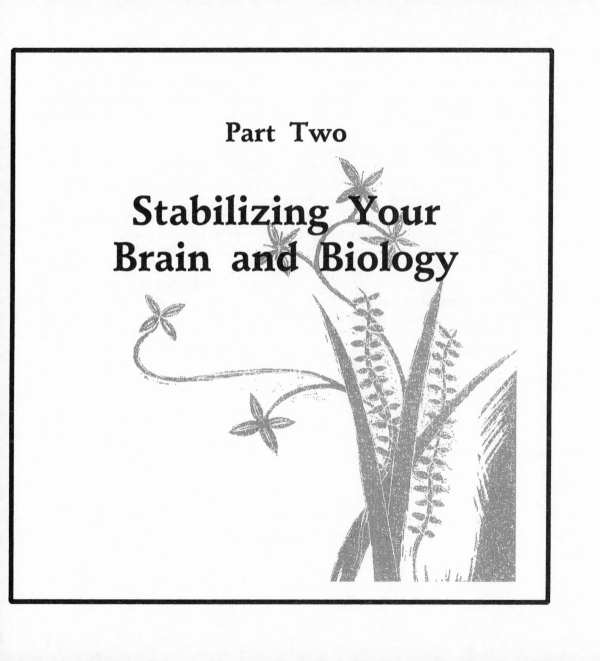

Part Two

Stabilizing Your Brain and Biology

For about 75 percent of people suffering from depression, biology is radically altered. This is manifest in significant hormonal changes, disruption of brain chemistry, and numerous physical symptoms such as disturbed sleep, fatigue, and loss of sex drive.

Sometimes depression is directly caused by metabolic problems in the brain or hormonal system. However, for many people, biological symptoms have been set in motion by exposure to serious life stresses. All mammals, people included, if exposed to prolonged stress, will at some point begin to experience altered biology and brain functioning. This is most pronounced when exposed to painful losses or to stresses that lead to a feeling of helplessness or powerlessness.

Until disordered biology is once again normalized, depression can continue on its relentless course. Modern treatment for depression often includes antidepressant medications, which have a solid track record of effectiveness in reducing certain depressive symptoms. This is a direct way to alter brain chemistry and restore normal biologic functioning. We'll address this briefly in a later chapter. Part 2 of this book, however, offers a number of very helpful, nonmedical approaches to stabilizing biology and reducing depression.

Chapter Four

Potent Solutions for Improving Sleep

Most people experiencing depression have disordered sleep. Insomnia is common; especially two types of insomnia: waking up frequently during the night, and early morning awakening (for example, waking up at 4 A.M. and being unable to return to sleep). In addition, 70 to 80 percent of people who are depressed, even if there is no insomnia, have poor quality sleep. This is characterized primarily by an inability to get adequate *deep sleep*. When a person experiences night after night deprived of deep sleep, three problems result (or intensify): exhaustion and fatigue during the day, impaired ability to think clearly (forgetfulness and poor concentration), and increased emotional sensitivity (becoming more easily frustrated and overwhelmed or developing a tendency to take things personally).

Many experts agree that disordered sleep is at the heart of the biological changes seen with depression and may ultimately be *the* main cause for a number of depressive symptoms.

Changes in brain chemistry likely are the starting place for sleep disorders in depression. However, a number of other factors including caffeine intake, drug and alcohol consumption, and a lack of physical exercise almost always make it worse.

The most common way people (depressed or not) try to combat fatigue is to increase consumption of caffeine. Among depressed people, caffeine use is often extraordinary.

Caffeine is notorious for interfering with the ability to fall asleep. But what most people do not know is that even moderate amounts of caffeine (that is, more than 250 milligrams per day) can seriously erode away deep sleep (which is already in short supply for people who are depressed). This is the case even if it does not cause problems in falling to sleep. So the unknowing person, by consuming caffeine, is inadvertently throwing gas on the depression fire!

Here are four important steps to take to begin improving your quality of sleep tonight.

- **Step One:** Take stock of your caffeine consumption. Starting tomorrow keep a running tally of your caffeine intake, using the following as a guideline: 6 ounces of coffee: 150 mg of caffeine; 6 ounces of decaf coffee: 5 mg; 6 ounces of tea: 50 mg; 12 ounces of caffeinated soda: 50 mg. Also watch for caffeine in medicines, for example: Excedrine: 65 mg; Anacin: 32 mg; Midol: 132 mg per pill. And, unfortunately, one chocolate candy bar: 20 mg.

- **Step Two:** Interpret your results. Caffeine levels beyond 250 mg (even if only consumed in the morning) may result in diminished deep sleep. Please note, many antidepressants actually increase the time caffeine stays in the blood stream. Thus, if you are taking antidepressants, amounts over 150 mg per day may disrupt sleep.

- **Step Three:** To reduce caffeine levels effectively, it's wise to gradually reduce intake (rapid reductions often cause caffeine withdrawal, with symptoms like anxiety, headaches, and insomnia). Thus, gradual tapering is important. What works best is to reduce caffeine levels by 25 percent per week. For example, someone drinking four six-ounce cups of coffee a day would begin by replacing one cup a day with decaf, and continue with this for a week before again reducing by an additional cup.

- **Step Four:** If you are experiencing marked fatigue but no anxiety, it may be possible to reduce caffeine use to 150 mg per day, making sure caffeine use is only in the morning. If you are experiencing any amount of anxiety, agitation, or restlessness, the ideal goal would be the complete elimination of caffeine.

If you are like a lot of people, you may be thinking that simply reducing caffeine couldn't really help reduce depression. It seems too simple! It's important to keep in mind that numerous and complex biological events occurring during sleep are essential for restoring normal brain functioning. The choice to begin caffeine withdrawal is a decisive step toward restoring your normal biological processes and is often tremendously beneficial. But it takes a few weeks. This takes us to problem number two:

The first week or two of caffeine reduction can be accompanied by increased fatigue. For many people this is very difficult. The best strategy to combat fatigue is to increase physical exercise (although it need not be strenuous—even walking more can help) and increase exposure to bright light. Exercise and bright-light exposure are natural stimulants. (We'll talk more about each in later chapters.)

Now that you're more aware of the first step to take, reducing caffeine intake, we're ready to address the problem of alcohol and drug use. In an attempt to reduce stress and to fall asleep more easily, many people turn to alcohol, tranquilizers, and sleeping pills. Such solutions are seductive because these drugs do, in fact, create drowsiness and can help people fall asleep. However, there are three very serious problems that often occur with these aids: 1. although they promote drowsiness, all of these drugs actually *decrease* the amount of time spent in deep sleep; 2. all can become habit forming; and 3. all have been shown to *increase* depression!

If you have been relying on alcohol, tranquilizers, or sleeping pills to get to sleep, *do not* stop abruptly (dangerous withdrawal symptoms can occur). Rather, speak with your doctor or therapist to find out how to safely reduce use of these drugs. (Please note: Antidepressant medications are *not* tranquilizers. Antidepressants actually have been shown to increase time spent in deep sleep.)

Finally, more than two decades of research have shown that regular exercise can increase deep sleep and, in general, improve the quality of sleep. We will explore exercise in greater detail in a later chapter.

Chapter Five

Improving Sleep: Shutting Off a Busy Brain

Deep in the brain is a nerve center for activation of the nervous system. Throughout the day, this region of the brain sends alerting stimulation to the brain at large and helps people remain awake and alert. At bedtime, it's necessary for this nerve center to reduce its activity as the brain gradually shuts down excitability; this is essential for the ability to fall to sleep and for entering states of deep sleep.

Four things can keep this brain center activated in the late evening and thus interfere with sleep: 1. activation from a "busy brain"—stressful thoughts and worries; 2. stimulation from the body—nerve messages coming up the spinal cord from the body (most commonly produced by either muscle tension or physical pain); 3. stress hormones that continue to circulate throughout the body; and 4. stimulating drugs.

To most effectively improve sleep, it's important to approach the problem from all four perspectives. We talked about reducing stimulating drugs in the last chapter. In this chapter, we will begin by discussing ways to shut off a busy brain (reducing stimulation from above).

Many people have tried to quiet their busy brains by counting sheep. The concept of counting sheep is sound; after all, what could be more boring than to count sheep? Replacing stressful thoughts with boring ones can reduce arousal, but the sheep-counting approach often just doesn't work. Why? When people are intensely preoccupied with stressful life events, it could be difficult to shut off these thoughts long enough to even imagine a sheep.

A more effective approach is to read a boring book or watch a boring TV show. These are external stimuli that can, at times, pull one's thoughts away from worries. If this works, great. However, for many, even this is not terribly effective. Two other approaches hold more promise.

Not infrequently, worrisome thoughts are sparked by stressful interactions or conflicts with others in the hours prior to bedtime (such as an argument with your children or spouse, or an anxiety-ridden discussion about finances). A helpful strategy is to avoid getting into arguments or conflicts later in the evening. This might best be approached by speaking with family members ahead of time and making an agreement that any troublesome issues should be discussed earlier in the day. This also should apply to the discussion of all emotionally loaded topics, such as finances, work stresses, problems with the kids, and so forth. Such important discussions can just as easily be scheduled for earlier in the day.

Please, once again, do not dismiss this strategy as being overly simplistic or trivial. What we're talking about is the restoration and preservation of sleep: a critical step in combating depression.

Another powerful technique has been shown by studies over the past ten years to be surprisingly effective. The technique involves back-and-forth eye movements. This approach takes two minutes, it's painless, and it is thought to rapidly reduce stress by disrupting and shutting off repetitive thoughts.

Often without wanting to or choosing to think about stressful things, thoughts automatically whiz through a person's mind. Some researchers have hypothesized that there are neural circuits or loops in the brain that get activated and appear to reverberate. The result is repetitive, troublesome thoughts that seem to serve little useful purposes and that generate stress and interfere with sleep. The eye-movement technique described below can often shut off such recurrent thoughts and may do so by some direct effect on neural circuits. Here's how it works.

- **Step One:** Sit in a comfortable chair and take a moment to relax. Then, while holding your neck and head still, begin moving your eyes from side to side (as if watching the ball go back and forth in a Ping-Pong™ game), taking about one second to shift your eyes from right to left and back to the right.

- **Step Two:** Repeat this back-and-forth movement about twenty times. Then stop, close your eyes and relax.

- **Step Three:** For a moment, scan through your body and simply be aware of any particular sensations of tension or discomfort. Simply notice it.

- **Step Four:** Repeat step one; take a calming, deep breath, and then begin back-and-forth eye movements. When finished, close your eyes and relax. A few seconds later, do it again, a third time. Most people will notice a calming of mental activity and a feeling of relaxation.

- **Step Five:** After going through this exercise a few times, you'll likely get the hang of it. Thereafter you can do eye movements as you get into bed at night, repeating them two or three times. Some people find that they can eventually achieve the same results by doing the eye movements even with their eyes closed.

This approach (especially when combined with the relaxation exercise in the next chapter) is often quite effective in promoting drowsiness and sleep. Additionally, eye movements can also be used during the day to reduce stress and promote tension reduction.

I wouldn't be surprised if this technique sounds pretty weird to you. It certainly did to me when I first heard about it. However, eye movements as an anxiety-reduction technique have caught on among many mental health therapists and currently are the focus of intense study by neuroscientists.

One thing that is good about this approach is that, when positive results occur, they generally are immediately noticed. Try it even once and see how it works for you.

Note: Those who wear contact lenses are advised to remove contacts before using eye movement techniques.

Chapter Six

Improving Sleep:
Calming the Body

Often times, muscle tension is very noticeable and even painful. However, it's a surprising fact that even significant muscle tension often becomes so pervasive, common, and continuous that people can actually get used to it, failing to really notice it after a while. It can be present every minute, even when you're asleep. Aside from the discomfort of tension headaches and tense necks and shoulders, it also can be a major contributor to poor sleep.

In this chapter we will take a look at a very effective muscle relaxation exercise. However, first a word or two about relaxation. Many (if not most) people going through very stressful times have been given this form of useless advice: "Just relax." Such counsel is about as helpful as telling a depressed person to "Just cheer up."

It may be hard to will yourself into a state of relaxation. However, one particular systematic procedure has been shown to effectively reduce muscle tension, even in highly stressed individuals. The technique accomplishes this largely by mechanically manipulating tense muscles. Here is how it works.

During times of stress, particular muscles and muscle groups tend to become tense automatically. Progressive muscle relaxation techniques are designed to reduce tension in all the body's major muscle groups.

The relaxation procedure requires a period of time when you will not be disturbed. Sit in a comfortable chair or recline on a couch, bed, or on a carpeted floor. Close your eyes and take two slow, deep breaths. As you exhale slowly, notice the gradual release of tension in your chest and shoulder muscles. Feel the weight of your body against the chair (couch, floor) and the gentle pull of gravity as you settle into the chair. After a few moments, you can begin a series of simple exercises, tensing particular muscles, holding the tension for a count of three and then releasing. Each time you tense and then release, you can enhance the effect by paying special attention to the experience of relaxation and letting go that occurs immediately after release.

Allow ten or fifteen seconds between each muscle group before proceeding to the next. The tensing exercises begin with the feet and progress like this:

1. Feet/toes

2. Calves/lower legs

3. Thighs

4. Buttocks (squeeze together)

5. Abdomen

6. Lower back (arch)

7. Chest (hold in a deep breath)

8. Hands (make fists)

9. Upper arms

10. Shoulders (shrug)

11. Face (squeeze eyes and purse lips)

12. Face (open eyes and mouth)

Many experts on relaxation techniques recommend ten to fifteen minutes twice a day to go through this exercise, especially when you're first learning the procedure. It is best to take plenty of time when first learning the procedure. However, after about a week, many people find that they can move through the various muscle groups more quickly, reducing the time it takes to four to five minutes.

Another effective way to reduce muscle tension will come as no surprise: soaking in a tub of hot water. This easy way to reduce tension can also be a pleasant way to be good to yourself (an important theme we will revisit later in this book).

Remember, tense muscles keep the brain on alert and interfere with sleep. These techniques directly shut off this source of arousal, loosening the muscles and calming the breath.

Chapter Seven

Improving Sleep: Lowering the Levels of Stress Hormones

All states of depression are accompanied by heightened levels of stress hormones (adrenaline, cortisol, norepinephrine), which are secreted by certain glands and circulate throughout the body. Some of these are directly responsible for physical symptoms, such as high blood pressure, insomnia, and muscle tension. And as mentioned earlier, when stress hormones traveling through the blood stream arrive at the activation center in the brain stem, they can keep these areas stimulated and can thereby interfere with sleep.

What makes these hormones start traveling? Well, exposure to distressing events certainly can activate the release of stress hormones. But it's also important to know that a number of other things that are not necessarily unpleasant can turn on these hormones as well. These include:

- Physical exercise

- Bright lights

- Noise

- Watching exciting TV, movies, sporting events, or reading exciting books

- Snacks that contain high levels of protein

Obviously, resolving significant life stresses and avoiding intense emotional interactions in the evening will ultimately make a difference in reducing the activation of stress hormone levels. Once activated, it may take two hours for such stress hormones to metabolically break down and be reduced to lower levels. Beyond this, the following suggestions can make a difference as well.

Exercise. In a later chapter we will look at the many advantages of exercise in the treatment of depression. But it's important to understand that any moderately intense exercise should not take place during a period of time three hours before bedtime. Exercise closer to bedtime can add to levels of stress hormones in the body.

Bright lights and noise. These sources of activation can stimulate the brain and may be helpful in combating fatigue and depression in general. However, during the evening hours, we need to prepare the brain to move into a shut-down mode. Lowering the lights two hours before bedtime can help. Likewise, loud noises should be reduced later in the evening.

Excitement. A common source of entertainment is watching television and movies or reading good books. Depressed people absolutely need to insert as much joy into their lives as possible. However, even if entirely enjoyable, intensely exciting shows, books, and sporting events do, inadvertently, increase stress hormone levels (and thus can interfere with sleep). Schedule exciting movies for weekend afternoons and carefully select more calming entertainment for the evenings (interesting but non-exciting TV or relaxing music).

Snacks. In the next chapter we'll take a closer look at diet. For now, let me just note that evening snacks that contain primarily protein (not accompanied by carbohydrates) can actually increase brain activity and may interfere with sleep.

Chapter Eight

You Are What You Eat: Dietary Solutions

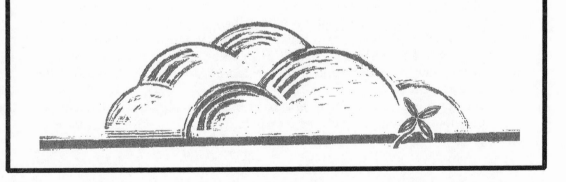

Brain chemistry depends, in part, on the availability of certain *essential amino acids*. These molecules, which must be derived from your diet, are the building blocks of key brain chemicals (such as serotonin, dopamine, and norepinephrine). A substantial body of research has supported the fact that many people suffering from depression have diminished levels of one or more of these important brain chemicals.

A normal, reasonably healthy diet generally supplies adequate amino acids for the body, although these molecules (owing to their size and chemical properties) only cross into the brain in fairly small amounts. The primary strategy in using dietary approaches to treating depression is to increase the amount and availability of selected amino acids in the brain.

Depressed people often slack off on their healthy eating habits. There are frequently substantial increases in the intake of junk food, fatty foods, caffeine, alcohol, and sugar, all of which can eventually contribute to health problems. At the very least, every effort should be made to eat a basically healthy diet.

Beyond this, you may find that specific dietary approaches may make a noticeable change in your mood. The two target symptoms for dietary "treatment" are: 1. anxiety (restlessness, tension, agitation, difficulty falling asleep) and 2. fatigue (lethargy, exhaustion, no energy, no motivation, impaired concentration).

Before we get to specifics, I'd like to point out that there are limitations to dietary strategies. First, not everyone responds. For some, the effects are substantial and ultimately very helpful. But for others, there may be no noticeable effects. People vary a lot in terms of their individual biology and metabolism. There is simply no way to know ahead of time if this will be effective for you. But it's a simple experiment to conduct, and if the approaches work, you should feel the difference right away.

Limitation number two: these approaches are "quick fixes." They do not cure depression, although they can be successfully used on a day-to-day basis as you wage your war on depressive symptoms.

Targeting anxiety. One of the most important brain chemicals for regulating mood is serotonin. With increases in serotonin, anxiety often diminishes. The amino-acid building block for serotonin is tryptophan. Generally a normal diet provides adequate amounts of tryptophan to the blood stream—the trick is getting it into the brain. One way to facilitate the entry of tryptophan into the brain is to increase insulin. With increased insulin, a window opens into the brain and tryptophan can more easily enter. An effective way to increase insulin is to eat carbohydrates. For this to work, the snack or meal should ideally include low glucose carbohydrates such as beans, some grains, peaches, apples, bran, pears, cherries, grapes, plums, and oranges.

Simple carbos like sugars and some starches can produce a very temporary improvement in mood (one reason that people often choose such snacks). But this is often followed by a sugar "crash," causing an intensification of anxiety and depression (plus, of course, lots of calories and weight gain). Avoid the following: donuts, French fries, candy, and (unfortunately) chocolate (I hate having to deliver that bit of bad news). One exception is if you eat simple carbohydrates and follow it with vigorous exercise. However, the intensification of negative mood can often be avoided by simply following carbohydrate consumption with vigorous exercise.

Targeting fatigue. The brain chemicals that increase energy and mental alertness are dopamine and norepinephrine. Both require the amino acid tyrosine as a building block. Proteins (and one of its amino acids, tyrosine) have been used for a number of years by the armed forces as a way for pilots to maintain energy and alertness. However, for this strategy to work, the protein snack needs to be eaten alone or with only a very small amount of carbohydrates (if proteins are eaten along with substantial amounts of carbos, the energizing effect is lost). The best proteins include: protein powder, eggs, fish, chicken, turkey, Gouda cheese, Monterey jack cheese, American cheese, and beef. Be careful not to eat protein snacks too close to bedtime since the increased energy and alertness can, at times, interfere with sleep.

One dietary option currently holds promise for providing more long-term effects on mood: omega-3 fatty acids. Preliminary studies have suggested a lower incidence of mood disorders in cultures that have omega-3 fatty acids as a regular part of their diets. Some promising studies at the National Institutes of Health tend to support the finding that treatment with supplemental dietary omega-3 fatty acids can reduce mood swings in depressed and manic-depressive patients. Omega-3 is a critical ingredient in nerve cell membranes, and a diet including this amino acid may actually help repair or build healthy brain cells.

This dietary approach does not produce a rapid change in mood, but rather is usually successful after several weeks to several months of the new diet. The best sources of omega-3 fatty acids are fish and fish oil. Flaxseed oil may also be helpful in stabilizing mood.

Chapter Nine

Over-the-Counter
Options

The use of herbal products and other so-called "natural remedies" have become increasingly popular in recent times. You may have considered this approach yourself. Before discussing specific options for treating depression, several cautions are warranted.

Cautions and Limitations

There are three main precautions regarding the use of over-the-counter (OTC) products to treat depression.

- *Not all OTC products are created equal.* Since herbal and other OTC products are not monitored by the Food and Drug Administration, there are no uniform standards for either quality or strength. Even though certain products may claim to have a particular milligram dosage, there are instances in which some products actually have little active ingredient. Thus, it's important to purchase OTC medications from reputable health food stores, or buying products manufactured by well-established pharmaceutical companies (many of the more well-known drug companies have gotten into the herbal business in recent years).

- *Not all OTC products are safe.* Although most are safe if taken as directed or taken alone, excessive doses can cause problems. Also, many serious difficulties can arise if OTC drugs or herbals are taken by people taking prescription drugs. There can be significant, and sometimes dangerous, drug interactions. Always consult with your physician or pharmacist when taking herbals along with other medications.

- *The choice to treat yourself with OTC products may interfere with seeking professional treatment.* It's not uncommon for people experiencing severe depression to attempt self-treatment with OTC drugs instead of seeking professional treatment, which could be more potent and effective.

OTC Products Effective in Treating Depression

The following products have some research support as effective treatments for depression.

- **St. John's Wort (hypericum):** May be effective in treating mild-to-moderate depression. Typical dosing ranges from 900 to 1800 mg per day. It generally takes six weeks of treatment before the first signs of improvement are noted. St. John's Wort appears to have few side effects; it is non-habit forming and well tolerated. St. John's Wort should *not* be taken at the same time one is taking prescription antidepressants. Dangerous interactions can occur. Additionally St. John's Wort can cause drug interaction problems with the following medications: warfarin, theophylin, digoxin, birth control pills, and drugs used to treat AIDS and migraine headaches.

- **SAM-e:** May be effective in treating mild-to-severe depression. There are few side effects; it is non-habit forming and well tolerated. Doses range from 400 to 1600 mg per day. Some improvement in symptoms can be seen after four weeks of treatment. SAM-e should always be taken with a vitamin-B complex supplement.

OTC Products That *May* Be Effective

- **5-HTP (5-hydroxytryptophan):** May be effective in treating mild-to-severe depression. There are few side effects, and it is non-habit forming and well tolerated. The typical daily dose is 300 mg and some symptom improvement may be seen within two to three weeks.

- **Kava Kava:** Can reduce anxiety and insomnia. Generally well tolerated. Kava kava can (at high doses) cause intoxication, drowsiness, and impaired alertness. It may be habit forming, although this has not been adequately researched.

Potentially Problematic OTC Products

- **Valerian Root:** This potent, sedating herb can aggravate depression and should not be used by those with depression.

- **Melatonin:** Low doses (0.5 mg taken at 6 P.M.) may help to improve sleep. However, many currently available melatonin products typically come in 1, 2, or 3 mg sizes. These higher doses may aggravate depression.

If you are using OTC products, be sure to inform your physician, pharmacist or therapist.

Chapter Ten

Catch Some Rays:
Bright Light Therapy

All animals studied, from snails to humans, have shown that certain environmental stimuli can have a powerful influence on internal biological processes, affecting hormone levels, body temperature, sleep cycles, activity levels, and brain chemistry. Most anthropologists agree that the human race first emerged in equatorial Africa some two to three million years ago. For hundreds of thousands of years, primitive humans lived and evolved in this ecological niche that is characterized by twelve hours of sunlight, three hundred sixty-five days per year. Across eons, all species must biologically adapt to local environmental conditions to survive, and this undoubtedly occurred for our ancient ancestors. There is a growing body of research suggesting that bright light stimulation does have a significant impact on the functioning of the human brain (our brains likely evolved over the millennia accustomed to getting twelve hours per day of such stimulation). And it appears that maintaining normal levels of brain chemicals, such as serotonin, has come to rely, in part, on getting a certain amount of bright light stimulation each day.

Most of us, these days, are exposed to substantially less than twelve hours a day of bright light. And for about 10 percent of us, this decreased light can contribute to depression. For some, reduced light exposure creates low energy and mild mood changes, but for others, it can provoke serious depressions, commonly referred to as seasonal affective disorder. As the name of the disorder implies, this depression is often associated with the decreased light exposure seen during winter months. However, it's also commonly seen in people who routinely work night shifts.

Light therapy may be the solution. The key to successful light therapy has nothing to do with light hitting the skin, but actually with light entering the eye. Light energy entering the eye and striking the retina activates a nerve pathway that penetrates deep into the brain. It is here that the stimulation influences levels of neurotransmitters, especially serotonin.

Bright light exposure can be accomplished by two means. One is by purchasing and using a commercially available "light box" (companies selling these products are listed below). The second approach is by getting exposure to sunlight—going outdoors.

How much exposure is required? The length of exposure varies tremendously from one individual to another. For some people, as little as ten minutes per day is all that is needed. Others may require up to ninety minutes.

If you've considered using a light box, it is essential to have adequate light energy. This requires boxes that emit a minimum of 2500 lux of light energy and for you to sit within two-and-a-half feet of the light source. Those who use light boxes often read or pay bills at a desk while seated before the light box. Please note, aside from commercially available light-therapy boxes, other sources of indoor lighting are simply not able to provide adequate light intensity.

If you prefer to try out natural sunlight, be sure to use sunscreen to avoid excessive UV ray exposure: remember, all that is required is light entering the eyes. And leave the sunglasses off!

Bright light exposure can have other benefits as well. First thing in the morning, bright light exposure can help you feel more energized. It may also help to normalize sleep patterns. Early morning light exposure is especially helpful if it is combined with exercise (for example, taking a short walk outdoors).

There are some cautions you should be aware of. Light therapy can sometimes produce mood changes in a few days, and it's generally free of side effects. However, it's important to note two precautions. The first is, if you have bipolar (manic-depressive) disorder or a history of bipolar disorder in your family, do not use light therapy without a doctor's advice. In such individuals, light therapy can occasionally trigger a manic episode. Also, bright light exposure may not be safe for individuals with certain eye disorders. (If you suffer from any diseases of the eye, please consult with your eye doctor before using light therapy.)

Light Box Companies

- ETA Systems: (800) 321-6699
- Northern Light: (800) 236-0066

Chapter Eleven

Light My Fire:
Restoring Sex Drive

Depression often completely eliminates sexual desire. Decreased sexual interest certainly may be due to a number of factors, such as having serious relationship conflicts and problems. However, the decreased sex drive seen in most cases of depression can occur in people who have very positive, loving relationships. Changes in brain chemistry that accompany depression are often the culprit.

It's really important for your significant other to realize the biological impact of depression on sex drive. Otherwise, they may misinterpret the decreased sexual interaction as stemming from some problem in the relationship.

Typically, depression must subside in order for sex drive to truly come back on line. So, you must be patient and understanding. However, it's important to note that the main aspect of sexual functioning derailed by depression is sexual desire. Many depressed people may be very disinclined to spontaneously feel sexual needs or to initiate intimate interactions. However, they may find that if their partner initiates sexual contact and is patient and not demanding, sexual feelings may then begin to come alive. In a sense, desire is in hibernation and loving physical contact may awaken it.

There is only one way to see if this works for you, and that is to go ahead and try it. I'd like to strongly suggest that you first have an open discussion with your partner beforehand. Talk about how depression has, for the time being, changed your sex drive and speak about how it may be helpful for them to take responsibility for initiating sexual contact, for the time being.

Chapter Twelve

The Role of Exercise in Reducing Depression

Anthropologists have determined that early humans, surviving by hunting and gathering, had to be moderately physically active for about two hours per day. This was true for the earliest humans, it persisted for several million years, and has changed only in very recent times. Especially during the past century, Americans have become increasingly sedentary.

Depression is rare among those who exercise frequently. Researchers have established that regular exercise increases levels of brain neurotransmitters, such as serotonin and norepinephrine, as well as the morphine-like chemical, beta-endorphin.

Exercise has both immediate effects (following moderate exercise, mood can improve for about one to one and a half hours) and long-term effects (more substantial changes in mood can be realized after ten weeks of regular exercise). In a review of the world literature on the impact of exercise on depression, Professor Larry Leith has found that 80 percent of studies report significant reductions in depression following exercise. Dr. Leith offers the following, specific recommendations.

How intense must a workout be? Intense, aerobic exercise does not appear to produce substantially better overall outcomes than mild-to-moderate intensity exercise (like walking).

How often should I exercise and for how long? Three times a week for a period of fifteen to thirty minutes may help to reduce depression. Additionally, daily walking for ten to twenty minutes can be helpful.

Rhythmic movements and reduction of anxiety and depression. Interestingly, repetitive, rhythmic movements often help to reduce anxiety and agitation. Such movements can be accomplished through exercise (weight lifting, jogging, or walking), but also may be as simple as gum chewing, knitting, or rocking.

The big hurdle. Exercise may be the single most potent strategy for defeating the biological aspects of depression. But let's be honest—it can be very difficult to get motivated to go and exercise. In my experience, the only viable approach to this problem is to hire a trainer at a sports club or enlist a "buddy" to join you, to encourage you, and to insist that you follow through. If you can start a program of regular exercise and stick with it, the benefits can be enormous. You'll not only reduce your depression, but will improve your overall health, enhance the quality of your sleep and increase your feelings of self-esteem.

Additional benefits of exercise. Beyond the positive effects on mood, exercise has been shown to also improve health by: decreasing cholesterol, decreasing blood pressure, improving circulation, reducing constipation, promoting weight loss or the prevention of weight gain, enhancing pain tolerance, reducing anxiety and muscle tension, and improving the quality of sleep.

Chapter Thirteen

Combating Fatigue

Fatigue associated with depression can be overpowering. It's unpleasant, it interferes with work or school, and it contributes to withdrawal and emotional paralysis. Approaches for combating fatigue have been addressed in several of the previous chapters. However, here I'd like to offer a review and an "energize yourself" checklist (strategies aimed at restoring energy and combating fatigue).

Upon awakening:

- Get up, and once up, do not lie back down (no matter what!).

- Eat a protein-rich breakfast with little or no carbs.

- Shower and dress.

- Keep caffeine use at a minimum.

- Energize yourself with one-to-two minutes of stretching.

- Take a ten-to-fifteen-minute walk outside.

- Get bright light exposure during your walk.

During the day:

- Keep involved with others.

- At all costs, avoid lying down during the day.

- Avoid naps (most times naps will actually *increase* fatigue and lower mood in people who are depressed).

- Eat a mid-afternoon protein snack.

- Choose the late afternoon for more intense exercise.

In the evening:

- A meal higher in carbohydrates may promote relaxation as you begin to wind down prior to bedtime
- Use sleep-enhancement approaches outlined in the previous chapters

Chapter Fourteen

Making the Most of Antidepressant Medication Treatment

A complete discussion of antidepressant medication treatment is beyond the scope of this book. For a more comprehensive overview of medical treatments for depression, please see *Consumer's Guide to Psychiatric Drugs*, by Preston, O'Neal, and Talaga, New Harbinger Publications, Oakland, California.

However, I would like to briefly outline a few critical issues that relate to successful antidepressant treatment. If you are taking antidepressants, you might want to look over this part of the book to make sure your treatment is on the right track.

The Most Common Reasons for Failure of Antidepressant Treatment

- Doses prescribed are too low (doses must be in the "therapeutic range" to be effective, but are often prescribed, especially in primary care settings, at doses too low to be effective).

- Antidepressants almost always *must* be taken for two to four weeks before the first signs of symptom improvement. Almost 70 percent of people prescribed antidepressants stop taking the medications prior to the onset of positive effects (generally, people feel so pessimistic and hopeless that they simply stop taking the medicine prior to the first signs of improvement).

- Moderate-to-heavy daily alcohol use can interfere with the metabolism of antidepressants, causing them to be ineffective.

- Taking medications on a regular basis is essential. Of those taking antidepressants, about one third take them on a sporadic basis, and the treatment fails.

- Many people take antidepressants and do get a good response, but then stop the medication prematurely and relapse. Almost always, once the medications work to eliminate depressive symptoms, an *additional six months of treatment* is recommended to prevent acute relapse.

Additional Facts About Antidepressants

- Antidepressants are *not* addictive or habit forming.

- Antidepressants are *not* tranquilizers.

- Antidepressants are *not* "happy pills." They primarily reduce the biological symptoms of depression such as fatigue, reduced sexual drive, and sleep disturbances.

- Antidepressant medications work best if they are combined with psychotherapy and self-help strategies.

Antidepressant Names and Dosages

NAMES		
Generic	**Brand**	**Usual Daily Dosage Range***
imipramine	Tofranil	150–300 mg
desipramine	Norpramin	150-300 mg
amitriptyline	Elavil	150-300 mg
nortriptyline	Aventyl, Pamelor	75-125 mg
protriptyline	Vivactil	15-40 mg
trimipramine	Surmontil	100-300 mg
doxepin	Sinequan, Adapin	150-300 mg
maprotiline	Ludiomil	150-225 mg
amoxapine	Asendin	150-400 mg
trazodone	Desyrel	150-400 mg
fluoxetine	Prozac, Sarafem	20-80 mg
bupropion-S.R.	Wellbutrin-S.R.	150-300 mg
sertraline	Zoloft	50-200 mg
paroxetine	Paxil	20-50 mg
venlafaxine-X.R.	Effexor-X.R.	75-350 mg
nefazodone	Serzone	100-500 mg
fluvoxamine	Luvox	50-300 mg
mirtazapine	Remeron	15-45 mg
citalopram	Celexa	10-60 mg
reboxetine	Vestra	4-8 mg
MAO INHIBITORS		
phenelzine	Nardil	30-90 mg
tranylcypromine	Parnate	20-60 mg

*   Ages 16–60. Over 60, doses are typically lower

Part Three

Reducing Negative Thinking

Regardless of the cause, all depressions result in negative thinking. Likewise, pervasive negative thinking always intensifies depression. Negative thinking takes many forms, but the most common are:

- **Pessimism and negative predictions about the future;** for example, "life is terrible and there is no hope for my future," or "I'll never get over this depression."

- **Excessively negative conclusions;** for example, "I am a failure at everything I do," or "Absolutely no one cares about me." These conclusions often *feel* accurate, but rarely are they 100% true.

- **Seeing only the worst and ignoring positives.**

- **Negative self-labeling;** for example, "I'm stupid," "I'm worthless," "I am a loser."

- **Excessive self-blame;** for example, "It's all my fault."

At times, such negative thinking is obvious, easy to spot, and hard to ignore. However, during depression *most* negative thinking is not in your conscious awareness. Rather, it is in the back of your mind, on the edge of awareness; like an almost silent voice constantly whispering, "Everything is terrible . . . it's hopeless . . . life will never be the same again."

If you tune in and really listen to this inner voice, you'll notice that it is almost constantly present. And, with each negative observation, each inaccurate or pessimistic conclusion, salt is rubbed into your depressive wounds. Many psychiatrists and psychologists believe that this unrelenting negative self-talk is the single most destructive aspect of depression owing to its ability to turn up the volume on despair and hopelessness.

Concerned friends may advise "Be positive," "Look on the bright side," or "Don't be so pessimistic." Good luck! Such advice, unfortunately, *never* helps to stem the tide of negative thinking. In this part of the book, however, we will look at potent strategies that work to control negative thinking, the most helpful of which is the "thought record."

Chapter Fifteen

The Most Powerful Strategy for Defeating Negativity: The Thought Record

Sara has been going through a time of significant depression following the breakup of a romantic relationship. One night, sitting alone in her apartment she became more and more depressed.

In the past few weeks she has had similar depressive experiences and each time felt helpless to do anything to ease her suffering. She'd often get into a downhill spiral of depression, feeling worse as the evening went on.

Various forms of the thought record have been developed and used since the late 1970s. This straightforward self-help technique generally requires about ten to fifteen minutes to complete, and often in this brief period of time intense negative feelings can be noticeably reduced. Try it even once and judge for yourself.

People who have never been truly depressed often suggest, "Don't be so negative," or, "Look on the bright side of life." These admonitions almost never help a person who is depressed. If people could somehow, by willpower alone, simply stop seeing things from a negative perspective, they would have done it long ago. Specialized strategies are required to alter negative thinking. It's important to emphasize that the thought record, described below, has nothing to do with the notion of "positive thinking." Rather, its goal is to keep your thinking *accurate* and *realistic* and to help you maintain perspective. This perspective includes clarity about both the positive and negative events or aspects of life.

Step one. Use your negative feeling (sadness, frustration, irritability, etc.) as a signal. Next time (or any time) you notice an especially intense, unpleasant feeling, let it serve as a cue to do a thought record (take this action rather than just endure the unpleasant emotion).

Step two. Briefly write down the emotion(s) you are feeling (sad, upset, angry, disappointed, discouraged . . .) in the "mood" column (see example on the next page), and next to the emotion, rate the intensity of the feeling (from 0, meaning the emotion is not present at all, to 100, meaning the worst you have ever experienced it in your entire life). Interestingly, simply rating the intensity of your mood, itself, has been shown to reduce emotional distress somewhat.

Step three. Reflect for a moment, and then ask yourself, "I am feeling _____ (sad, hopeless) right now. What is going through my mind?" Almost always, strong feelings are accompanied by or associated with underlying thoughts (although often we are not fully aware of thinking during moments of emotion unless a conscious effort is made to notice these thoughts). Intensely painful waves of emotion are typically accompanied by the kind of thoughts we listed in the introduction to part 3 (excessive self-blame or pessimistic predictions). Whatever thoughts come to mind, jot them down. To make this exercise effective but easy, write down your thoughts only briefly.

Let's see how Sara approached this technique. Instead of sinking into an increasingly depressed mood one evening, she decided to take action and use her thought record for the first time. She wrote the following:

Mood	Thoughts
Sad (75)	Tom left me for another woman.
Hopeless (80)	I'll never get over this depression.
	No one will ever want to be with me, and I'll be lonely for the rest of my life.

She was able to fairly easily pinpoint certain thoughts that were provoking her emotional pain and it only took her a couple of minutes to do this step.

Step four. Please note, this step can be emotionally difficult, but it is very important. The step requires honestly asking yourself for any and all proof that the thoughts noted in step 3 may be at least somewhat true. In other words, what evidence supports the thoughts. Let's see how Sara approached this:

Thoughts	Evidence Supporting the Thoughts
Tom left me for another woman.	This is accurate. He told me so, and I have seen him with her.
I'll never get over this depression.	There is no absolute evidence that I'll never get over my depression.
No one will ever want to be with me.	This is hard to know for sure.
I'll be lonely for the rest of my life.	I can't tell the future for sure.

Step five: Negative thoughts are compelling; they *feel* real, accurate, and certain. However, you must try to be very objective, and one way to do this is to ask yourself, as you write down your response, "Is this thought (or belief or statement) absolutely true? Is it the whole truth and nothing but the truth?"

Again, let me emphasize that this is not an exercise in positive thinking or an attempt to pretend that things are perfectly okay or to superficially cheer yourself up. The exercise is a search for the truth and for clarity and accuracy in your thinking. For Sara, a part of this ("Tom left me for another woman") is accurate, and it's painful. In contrast, the thought, "No one will ever want to be with me" may *feel* accurate to Sara, but it is not supported by any factual data. No one can really tell the future.

As you do step 5 ask yourself, "Is there any evidence that refutes or does not support my thoughts." Sara wrote the following:

Thoughts	Evidence Refuting
Tom left me for another woman.	Nothing refutes this. It is accurate.
No one will ever want to be with me.	Guys have asked me out in the past. There is no solid proof that, for some reason, it will never happen again.
I'll be lonely for the rest of my life.	I am lonely now, but I am a friendly person. I like people. In general, I know a lot of people that like me. There is no evidence that I will absolutely be lonely for the rest of my life.

Step six. Look back at what you have written. Look at the evidence in both columns and ask, "All things considered, how do I feel right now?" Then re-rate the intensity of your feelings. For Sara, it was: sad (65) and hopeless (35). She *is* sad, and she has every right to be. The breakup of a love relationship is a very painful experience. This reality needs to be faced and honored as an understandable and honest human emotion. However, Sara's overall level of distress was noticeably reduced, mainly due to decreased feelings of hopelessness. This exercise simultaneously helped her acknowledge her legitimate sadness and regain realistic perspective.

Well, maybe it helped Sara, but it won't help me. The thought record may seem too simplistic (at first glance, it does to most people who are depressed). It is very easy to simply dismiss this as another quick-fix tip characteristic of pop psychology. However, don't let its apparent simplicity deceive you. During the past twenty-five years, this approach has been shown to be one of the most useful techniques for correcting unrealistic negative thinking and for reducing depressive moods. The thought record has solid research support as an effective approach for treating depression.

When you're depressed, thinking clearly and accurately without using the thought record can be extremely difficult. The process of writing thoughts and evidence down and the ability to see your thoughts in black and white greatly facilitates the ability to clarify thinking and to gain realistic perspective.

Please give the thought record a try. Or if you are in therapy, it may be very helpful to spend part of a session and complete a thought record with the help of your therapist. For Sara, the alternative would have been to sink into yet another evening of depression, helpless to do anything to ease her pain. Using this approach she was able, in about fifteen minutes, to significantly alter her mood. No technique completely erases unpleasant feelings, but the name of the game with depression is taking action to gain some measure of control over your mood. Such action is the only realistic antidote to feelings of helplessness.

Chapter Sixteen

Beyond Paralysis

Craig has struggled with depression for months. On weekends he wakes up feeling fatigued and blue. Even though he knows that going out to shop at the store, going to a movie, or even mowing the lawn might be a good thing to do, he feels exhausted and unmotivated. He collapses on to the couch and stares at TV all day. By the end of the day, he thinks, "I wasted the day. I feel worse than I did when I woke up. My life is out of control."

Does this sound familiar? Pessimism is at the heart of feelings of hopelessness (thoughts like "I'll never get over this depression"). It is also one of the major factors that creates paralysis and the tendency to give in to inactivity. One factor that contributes to this is a pessimistic belief that, "Even if I forced myself to get up and out of the house, I'd be miserable. I wouldn't accomplish or enjoy anything, so why try?"

A simple exercise that often helps a lot is to complete a "Satisfaction Prediction Sheet" that has been suggested by the noted psychiatrist, David Burns (1999, 148). It takes only a minute to do. Here is how this works. Take a piece of paper and make three columns. In the first column, list your planned activities. Then, in the second, write down your prediction of the degree of satisfaction (the sense of pleasure or accomplishment) you anticipate *prior* to carrying out the activity. (0 meaning absolutely no satisfaction, 100 meaning very satisfying). Then, after you have completed an activity on the list, once again rate the satisfaction level, but this time base it on your actual experience. Craig's next Saturday looked like this:

Activity	Anticipated Satisfaction	Actual Satisfaction
Mow lawn	0%	25%
Trip to store, to purchase a CD	25%	50%
Eat lunch at favorite Mexican restaurant	25%	60%
Mail packages	0%	10%

Craig discovered, as do most people who try this exercise, that prior to actually engaging in activities, depression had the impact of casting a negative shadow of anticipation. Negative expectations create low motivation and ultimately greatly contribute to an ongoing sense of powerlessness. Yet often, once activities are underway, there is a much greater *actual* sense of satisfaction than was expected. And looking back at the Satisfaction Prediction Sheet often spurs motivation. So that the next time, it will feel somewhat easier to get motivated to pursue live activities. It's a motivation enhancing exercise!

Chapter Seventeen

Breaking the "Apathy Cycle"

Does this sound familiar? "I ought to get up and do something. I feel exhausted. I don't feel motivated. The hell with it." Then you collapse and do nothing.

For most people, a natural way to initiate action is to first think about what you want or need to do. The thoughts alone then have a tendency to generate their own energy; anticipating having fun or imagining the sense of satisfaction in completing a task can spark inner energy and ignite action. This feeling of energy or enthusiasm is what people call "feeling motivated." When you are not depressed, this strategy works well, most of the time. However, depression throws a wrench into the works. During times of depression, it's often almost impossible to anticipate things and then to feel motivated. The energy and enthusiasm simply is not there. Thus if you wait to feel motivated before taking action, it will never occur. This strategy does not work for people who are depressed.

The alternative is to not wait to feel motivated. Rather, to *just do it*. You must *push* yourself to get moving. Almost always, after a person has gotten up out of bed or off the couch, has gone outside and started to drive to the store, or to do other activities, *then* a shift begins to occur, and you feel at least somewhat more motivated. It's likely that a part of this result is due to the fact that physical movement in itself increases the brain chemicals serotonin and norepinephrine, so literally, movement creates energy. As Dr. David Burns has said, "Motivation follows action" (1999, 170).

A very helpful approach for those who find it extremely difficult to get started is to enlist the help of a friend or family member. It might be wise to have a talk with this person and say, "I am having a tough time getting up and getting started. I'd like you to help me by encouraging me, kicking me in the butt, and getting me started. I believe that once I'm up and about, it will be easier. Your help with this would be most appreciated." Another version might be, "I can't allow myself to stay in bed or on the couch all day. I need a jump start, and it would help me a lot if you would, if necessary, drag me out of bed, pester me, encourage me, or do whatever it takes to get me started. I think it will help me a lot." If the friend does not live with you, agree ahead of time to call them on

Saturday morning (or any other agreed upon time), after you are actually out and about. Feeling an obligation or commitment to touch base with a friend often is a helpful strategy.

Another way to energize into action. Craig would often think, "I need to get up and get going," but in such moments, he was acutely aware of physical feelings of heaviness and fatigue. The physical sensations contributed to his conclusion that he was unable to get up and get moving: "I just can't do it. I'm too tired." An additional useful technique to use is to take one minute and do simple stretching exercises, like touching your toes and stretching your arms toward the sky. These exercises require little or no effort and yet almost always produce an immediate sense of increased energy. Feeling a bit more energized for a couple of minutes after stretching can make it easier to get up and out the door. The boost in energy lasts only a minute or two; this is not a permanent solution. But in that moment of heightened energy, do not sit back down, do not lie down—rather, put one foot in front of the other and propel yourself out the door. By the time you are outside and in the car, it will feel better. Give this a try. It's simple, it's do-able, and it works.

A final strategy is, once you are outside, walk for two minutes. Walk down the street or around your house. This minimal amount of physical movement can further energize you, giving you enough motivation to launch you into the day.

Chapter Eighteen

Tyranny of the "Shoulds"

Some common "shoulds" include:

- "I should be stronger."

- "I shouldn't let things get to me so much."

- "I shouldn't be so sensitive."

- "I should be able to pull myself out of this depression."

- "This shouldn't be happening to me."

"Shoulds" and "shouldn'ts" are powerful, negative thoughts that convey a strong inner desire or an insistance that you, others, or reality ought to be a certain way. They also can represent a set of unrealistic standards for your own behavior. The failure to live up to such standards results in harsh judgments and a condemning of the self.

What is so important to appreciate is that at the heart of should statements is a perception of the world that always generates a sense of powerlessness. When you think with shoulds, you are always seeing yourself as a victim of circumstances beyond your control. This perception of "victimhood" contributes greatly to feelings of powerlessness and helplessness. Thinking with shoulds may be the most potent way that human beings inadvertently turn up the volume on misery.

This very common thought pattern, unfortunately, never really helps to change situations or to motivate people. Rather, it always becomes a source of harsh self-criticism and greatly intensifies feelings of helplessness.

The most helpful way to combat shoulds is to make use of your thought record. In moments of intense negative emotions, the question, "What's going through my mind?" often reveals shoulds.

Betsy's experience provides a good example. She had been feeling increasingly depressed, agitated, and upset with herself. Much of her depression centered around her growing marital conflicts and a great disappointment in her husband, who had become increasingly distant during the past two years.

Betsy finally sat down, calmed herself down a bit, and wrote out a quick thought record on a tablet of paper:

Mood	Thoughts
Upset (90)	
Frustrated (95)	How can he be so cold?
Angry (80)	
Hopeless (95)	It shouldn't be this way. Marriages should bring happiness not sorrow
Anxious (85)	I shouldn't be so upset . . . what's wrong with me?
Angry with myself (85)	

Note, often questions like, "How can he be so cold?" carry hidden "shoulds" ("He shouldn't be so cold").

The most powerful way to address shoulds in a thought record, is to rewrite your statement, but not in terms of shoulds. Rather, substitute the terms "I want" or "I don't want." Here is what Betsy wrote:

"I don't *want* it to be this way."

"I *wanted* my marriage to be happy."

"I *don't want* him to be cold toward me."

And instead of stating "I shouldn't be so upset," it is more helpful to simply state how you do feel:

"I *do* feel upset. This matters a lot to me, and God knows I *never wanted* things to turn out this way."

What is embedded in Betsy's revised statements are the following:

• She is acknowledging the truth of how she really feels.

• Rather than being harsh or critical of herself, she is adopting an attitude of understanding and compassion for herself.

Almost always when people use such an approach, one important result is to feel significantly less powerless, and often this is *immediately noticeable!* Try it even once and be the judge. When this is done, a shift occurs from viewing yourself as a victim to seeing yourself as a human being with legitimate emotional pain.

Shoulds are everywhere. On close inspection, almost invariably, all intense emotions are accompanied by shoulds. And shoulds always have the effect of taking any painful emotion and turning up the volume.

In my experience, the simple exercise described above is one of the most rapid ways to de-escalate very intense emotional upset and regain perspective and a sense of control over strong feelings. However, for this to be truly effective, you must also then give yourself permission to acknowledge and to experience the underlying, legitimate human emotions. For Betsy, it was clear and understandable that the emotional distance she has felt from her husband is a source of sadness and disappointment.

You should try this exercise, even once! (Sorry, I mean I *want* you to give it a try.)

Chapter Nineteen

Shame, Guilt, and Self-Blame

Ginny says, "Since I've been depressed, I've had this overwhelming feeling of worthlessness. I so often feel like I'm to blame for all the problems in my family . . . like it's all my fault."

A certain amount of guilt or feeling of responsibility is often appropriate. It's a sort of internal thermostat that tells us when we have transgressed others or inadvertently caused harm to another. However, the finger of blame can often become excessively harsh and unrealistic when you're in the throes of depression. Also during bouts of depression, there may be a tendency for you to assume more than your fair share of responsibility for problems that may in fact be due to a number of factors, including the actions of others.

Excessive, unrealistic self-criticism, and shaming always intensify misery and rarely help improve circumstances. If you are experiencing these feelings, try out the following:

Step one. Often the voice of self-blame is subtle and only on the edge of awareness. Thus it's important to first make this inner thinking conscious and clear. One of the best ways to do this is to take five minutes or so and write your self-critical thoughts down on paper.

- What do I think about myself?

- What am I telling myself?

- In what ways do I feel to blame?

- What things do I feel a sense of shame about?

Step two. In keeping with the thought record, next consider two things: Is there any solid evidence that you are directly to blame or any evidence that refutes this? As mentioned in earlier chapters, these questions are most effectively addressed by writing down such evidence, rather than just thinking about it.

Step three. Looking at the evidence in both columns, carefully reflect, and ask yourself, "Is this 100 percent true?", "Are there any other explanations, any other factors or other people who have contributed to the particular problems or events?" Without being overly critical of others, you can simply approach such questions in a matter-of-fact manner. The goal is not to attack or blame, but rather to find explanations. "Just the facts, ma'm . . ."

Step three. After a careful analysis of the facts in step three, if there clearly are mistakes you've made or inadvertent hurt caused to others, then consider the following ways of looking at it:

- It is often helpful to honestly "own" the part you may have played in creating hurt or problems, offering apologies when appropriate.

- Carefully consider your *intentions.* Often people never intend to hurt others or create difficulties. It became clear to Ginny that she did often ignore her children as she was working overtime in desperate pursuit of a job promotion. She wanted the promotion *and* she loves her kids. She honestly admitted to herself that she was away from her children to a degree that may have been emotionally hard on them. In this spirit of honesty she was also quite certain that, "I never intended to cause them any emotional pain. I just got overly focused on my job." This ability to own her part of the problem while making it clear and conscious that she had absolutely no intention to cause her children pain, helped Ginny turn down the volume on what had been intense self-blame and, at times, self-hatred.

- Change guilt to regret. Guilt often carries a dual message: feeling bad about something you have done *and* a sense of "badness of self." It is this second element that is often unwarranted and is the source of unrealistic self-loathing. An alternative is to give yourself permission to own and feel a sincere sense of regret, but move away from the more global sense of being defective or bad that guilt often implies.

- The experience of shame digs even deeper into one's sense of self: a self that is bad, unworthy, or deserving of scorn. Shame, in a sense, embodies a *global* and condemning view of yourself. Most people experiencing significant amounts of shame make such conclusions based on limited data. Such data may certainly include mistakes that have been made, some of which may have had a clearly negative impact on others. Yet typically, the shame conclusions fail to take into consideration a multitude of other data; for example, numerous times that the person has been kind, helpful, loving, and available to others.

If you are plagued by feelings of shame, it is *essential* to think carefully about yourself as a *whole* human being. This must involve honest acceptance of shortcomings, owning one's mistakes, and humbly acknowledging your membership in the human race where no one is without fault. But it is also very important to give careful consideration to other aspects of yourself and of your life.

Ginny took careful stock of herself and acknowledged things for which she felt regret. And then she also wrote the following list of personal attributes:

- I deeply care for my husband and children. If it were required, I know in my heart that I would die for them.

- I am a good and loyal friend.

- My friends and family trust me. I keep confidences and I follow through with promises.

- I may have made mistakes, but I know that I have never intentionally hurt other people.

- There are causes that I believe in. I contribute money to my church, and I speak out about things that I believe in.

- When my kids have needed me to take a stand on their behalf, I've done it and never let them down.

Without conscious effort and the specific technique outlined above, Ginny, and others like her, could continue for months to be eaten alive by the consuming, destructive force of shame.

Chapter Twenty

Finding Balance in a Negative World

It may be hard to believe, but studies have shown that depressed people actually see reality more clearly than those who are not depressed! This does appear to be true, but it needs some qualifications. What depressed people do see (often accurately) are negative events and aspects of life. In fact, changes in brain functioning occurring during depression are felt to underlie the tendency to become exquisitely aware of and sensitive to noticing bleak, pessimistic, and depressive things in the world. What nondepressed people do, generally, is to distort or tune out, to a large degree, awareness of negative things in the environment. In addition, nondepressed people are significantly more able to notice and to take in positive or happy events. Tuning out the negative, at least to a degree, and seeing the positive may be an essential ingredient in maintaining a positive mood.

Depression brings with it a view of the world that accentuates negativity and blinds one from really noticing beauty, love, positive interactions, and events that inspire hope and happiness. This is never intentional; it's always automatic. And it always increases misery.

A very important strategy to adopt when you are depressed is one that requires taking time to willfully and consciously acknowledge positive things in your life. I must emphasize that this is not an approach intended to gloss over serious problems; it is not an attempt to simply "look on the bright side of life." Rather, this approach is based on the two following assumptions: 1. it is natural during depression to focus almost exclusively on the negative; and 2. looking for positives is a way to achieve a more balanced and realistic view of life. Accurate and balanced perception (seeing *both* the positive and the negative) are central to maintaining perspective and regulating mood.

Consider the following suggestions for finding balance in what likely seems like a negative life.

Step one. Think back to when you were younger, when you yearned for things in your life such as a college degree, a profession, a loving relationship, a sense of freedom and independence in choosing a style of life, owning your own home, and so on. Remember how much you longed for these sought-after goals. Then, acknowledge the goals that have now been realized. Sit with this awareness for a while.

People often take goals that have been achieved for granted and lose sight of how important such things can be in one's life. This exercise in remembrance and reflection can often help you experience a greater sense of gratitude for goals achieved.

Step two. Throughout the day, as many times as possible, stop yourself for a second or two and consciously take stock of the moment. Intentionally focus on yourself and the environment in the here and now, and see if there is anything you can notice that is nice, sweet, beautiful, upbeat, humorous, or peaceful. For example, "Right this moment, I feel calm and there is a cool breeze," or you notice a beautiful tree, a blue sky, a smile on a child's face, a friendly or courteous interaction with a clerk at the grocery store, a great tasting lunch, a funny joke on a TV program, and so on.

Some depressed people may have thoughts like, "This is silly," "I don't feel in the mood to stop and smell the roses," or "How could this possibly help me get over this depression?" Also, this strategy may be something that simply does not dawn on you to do.

Like a lot of exercises and suggestions in this book, this particular suggestion, in itself, won't cure depression. But it is an action you can choose to do that can have an impact. One of my clients, Chuck told me: "I've realized that to get over this depression, I must adopt an attitude in which I am decent to myself, where I give myself permission to enjoy what I can and notice small positive things whenever I am able."

This approach is not Pollyannaish; you are not denying serious problems in your life. But you are willfully choosing to expand your vision of the world and strive for a more realistic and balanced perspective.

Step three. Each night, take one minute before bed and write in a diary, listing at least two things for which you feel grateful today. Then sit and reflect for a moment. Chuck did this as well, and told me, "When I look over my list of gratitudes, I remind myself that, especially when I am depressed, I cannot afford to ever forget these things in my life for which I feel grateful."

Step four. Scan the following list of positive statements (often referred to as affirmations), and see if any feel appropriate and sincere to you. The chanting of unauthentic affirmations rarely helps anyone who is seriously depressed. However, you may find that one or two of these do strike a positive chord. If so, it may be helpful to write them on an index card and, several times a day, pull it out and read it to yourself (even out loud, if you are alone).

These are words of encouragement and reassurance, and they are a way of providing ongoing support for yourself as you take action to defeat depression.

- I may not be perfect, but in this moment I am doing the best I can.

- I deserve to treat myself in a decent way.

- I am only human, and like others, I have strengths and limitations.

- I need to stick by my guns; believe in myself, take a stand, and hold on to things I believe in.

- I need to trust myself—trust my instincts and intuitions.

- Keep focused on what matters: don't get bogged down by trivial stuff or by others' opinions.

- It's okay for me to live life at my own pace.

- To thine own self be true: it's okay to live life in accord with my own values and beliefs.

- It is human to mourn losses.

- (For Christians) Even Jesus Christ wept tears of anguish when he faced very difficult times.

- I won't be so hard on myself.

Part Four

Combating Low Self-Esteem

Some people go through their entire lifetimes burdened by feelings of worthlessness, inferiority, and low self-esteem. Often, this is a natural outcome from being mistreated, unloved, unappreciated, unsupported, neglected, or abused as a child. However, many people may generally feel okay about themselves until depression hits. Almost invariably, depression takes a toll on self-esteem. This is manifested in a number of ways:

- Feeling inferior or inadequate

- Lacking self-confidence

- Indecisiveness (doubting your ability to make good decisions)

- Unrealistic or harsh self-criticism, self-blame, guilt, and shame

- Viewing yourself in a very negative light; seeing yourself as stupid, incompetent, ugly, unlovable, worthless

- Self-hatred

In this section of the book, we will look at some strategies for reducing low self-esteem.

Chapter Twenty-one

Getting Clear About
What Matters

Self-esteem for most of us certainly is influenced by the opinions of others. If we are valued by our boss, loved by our spouse, respected by colleagues, self-worth is bolstered. Conversely, being ridiculed, criticized, or belittled by others can be very emotionally wounding. Being the recipient of such negative messages from others may be a contributing cause of depression.

At times, critical remarks from others are simply an expression of differences of opinion or perspective. However, it's not uncommon for such words to be spoken out of anger or in an attempt to hurt or control another.

Julie's example is all too common: "My husband, Kevin, is constantly putting me down or looking at me with a 'God, you're stupid' expression on his face. It hurts a lot, and most times I find myself believing that his criticisms are true."

Depressed people often become very sensitive to even mildly critical comments, taking them to heart and feeling terribly hurt even when critical comments were not intended to be hurtful or even to be taken seriously.

Sometimes there is an absence of actual criticism coming from others. But depression can contribute to negative beliefs about the self, generated solely from within.

One way to strengthen yourself, to erect a buffer against criticism and to tackle the problem of low self-esteem is to find ways to clarify and strengthen inner values and beliefs. The following steps may help.

Step one. Get this idea clear in your mind: "I am separate from others. No law states that I must agree with everyone, and I have a right to find my own way through life, to discover what I truly believe to be important values, goals, and beliefs for myself. I can learn to respect others' opinions while also honoring my own. In many relationships, ideas, beliefs, and lifestyles may be different; neither one right nor wrong, but simply different. Human beings often do not see eye to eye."

Step two. Write down those things that you feel define who you are, the things that really matter to you. These may include some of the following areas of life:

What Matters to Me

- Things I hold to be important characteristics of good relationships (trust, openness, and so on)

- My spiritual values

- Values and beliefs that I hold so dearly that I would be willing to defend them with my life

- The people in my life that mean the most to me

- Social or political issues that matter to me

- Qualities that I require in a good friend or in an intimate relationship

- Activities that make my life enjoyable and worthwhile

- Small things that I enjoy

- My favorite places

- Things about me that other people value

Step three. Often in very old age, people develop a new perspective on life. Looking back over the years and coming closer to the end of life, many older and wiser people come to appreciate the folly in living life in accord with others' expectations. At some point in life, it simply doesn't matter that much anymore what other people think of you. Letting go of the pressure to conform or to please others, you may be better able to live more according to your own inner needs, values, and beliefs.

A useful exercise is to imagine yourself as a very old person, perhaps someone who has only a short time to live. Play with this image a bit—get into it enough to really experience how things might seem from such a perspective. Then ask yourself, "What things am I ready to let go of? What felt obligations can

I gratefully release? How does it feel to divorce myself from others' judgments and expectations?"

This exercise can help you more clearly connect with your more private and authentic self. It can also help to identify current sources of felt criticism or judgment.

Step four. Once you have clearly identified important beliefs and values, the next step is to focus on giving yourself support for being who you are. You have a right to live your life on your own terms, even if others may not fully agree. And you certainly have the right to suspend self-criticism and accept and honor your true self. As Popeye says, "I yam what I yam."

Often when people get depressed, they begin to lose contact with the self. Especially during difficult times, it's important to refresh your memory regarding your inner and unique self, to anchor yourself in your own beliefs, values, activities, and sources of enjoyment, and to embrace (rather than discount) these personal sources of meaningfulness and aliveness.

Step five. Finally, it can be helpful to make a list with two columns, one listing "Those who support me for who I am," and "Those who do not." Once this list is made, it might be good to consider the following metaphor. If you had a precious yet fragile family heirloom and you wanted to entrust it to someone for safekeeping, you wouldn't give it to just anyone, nor would you hand it over to someone who would damage or neglect it. You would choose someone whom you can really trust, someone who can appreciate the value and preciousness of the object. Likewise, it's a good idea to be careful about revealing yourself only to those whom you really trust. To whom do you entrust your private thoughts, feelings, needs, wishes, and fears? With whom is emotional vulnerability safe? When people are depressed and self-esteem is low, you need to surround yourself with companions who can appreciate and support you, not those who throw salt in the wound.

Chapter Twenty-two

Your Positive
Activity Diary

Annie is a thirty-five-year-old woman who came to therapy complaining of depression: "I can't get anything accomplished. I'm at home all day with the kids. By the time my husband gets home, the house is a wreck. I look at my house and think, 'What's wrong with me?' I don't even work. I'm just a housewife, and I can't get anything done. I feel out of control of my whole life!" Annie considered herself an inadequate mother and housekeeper, who "does nothing productive." Since she has three children, ages one, two, and four, it was hard for her therapist to believe her statements, "I don't even work," and "I can't get anything done."

The therapist asked Annie to start keeping an activity diary, at least for one day. She asked Annie to write down *everything* she did, even small things like picking up a toy or getting a drink for one of her children. She brought a small notebook with many pages filled to her next therapy session. She said, "I can't believe it! As I was writing everything down, it hit me. I'm continuously busy from morning 'til night. In fact, it was hard to keep up with the writing—I know I missed some things. Maybe my house looks like a wreck, but at least I know that I'm working my butt off. I *am* getting a lot done each day."

Especially if you are depressed, it's easy to overlook or minimize accomplishments. At the end of the day you may conclude, "The day was wasted. I got nothing done." This perception lowers self-esteem and can bring on a sense of defeat. An activity diary can help present a realistic view of events.

There are two ways you can do this. First, *write down every single activity* you do each day, as Annie did. This does take some time and is not practical for most of us on a regular basis. Still, doing it even for just a day or two can be helpful in providing you with evidence of your productivity, as it was for Annie. An additional practical approach for use on a daily basis is to *record the major events* of each day, briefly noting the following: *tasks completed* (or progress made toward completion); *positive events* (receiving a compliment, pampering yourself with a hot bubble bath, having a nice lunch with a friend, getting a letter, feeling good about a job well done); and *experiences* that matter to you (spending time with your child, gardening, writing a letter to a friend, saying a prayer).

This process works best if you keep it simple and easy. It is best to jot down only brief, three-to-five word statements. Then, review the list at the end of the day. Even very depressed people who feel as thought they have accomplished absolutely nothing in a day are often surprised to find out that in fact they've done many things and experienced some moments of pleasure. This approach is easy to put into action and can give immediate payoffs. It's an important way to combat feelings of helplessness and low self-esteem.

Chapter Twenty-three

Developing an Inner Language of Self-Support

As we've seen in previous chapters, internal thoughts (self-talk) often underlie a depressive mood. This is also true when it comes to low self-esteem. Whether it is obvious or subtle, inner voices of criticism, self-hatred, judgment, unrealistic standards, and condemnation always fuel the fires of low self-worth. Pay attention to your inner voice and see if any of the following statements might provide kinder, gentler, and more realistic support for yourself.

If you are thinking "I can't do anything right," consider these alternatives:

- I do a number of things right, and I also make mistakes.

- I am doing the best that I can at this moment.

- Accomplishing things is difficult for all people experiencing depression.

- Even if I am struggling, I should not lose awareness of the many difficulties I have faced and overcome before.

If you are thinking "I am just lazy and unmotivated," consider these alternatives:

- Motivation is hard to muster for everyone who is depressed.

- This is not a matter of laziness. This is a symptom of depression.

- Especially during a time of depression, it is important to not be hard on myself.

If you are thinking "I shouldn't be feeling so bad," consider this alternative:

- It is not a matter of shoulds or shouldn'ts. The fact is, I'm depressed, and when human beings go through depression, it is natural to experience strong, painful emotions.

If you are thinking "I should be better able to control my emotions," consider this alternative:

- Again, it's not a matter of shoulds or shouldn'ts. It's just a fact that I am having a difficult time now, and I am committed to doing whatever I can to overcome depression.

If you are thinking "My depression is a sign of personal weakness," consider these alternatives:

- Nonsense! As a person suffering from depression, I walk in the company of incredibly strong, capable people such as Abraham Lincoln and Winston Churchill (both of whom suffered from terrible depressions).

- In part, depression is due to biological changes. When body chemistry changes during a severe bout of the flu, is this seen as a sign of personal weakness? Of course not.

If you are thinking "I'll never get over this depression," consider this alternative:

- I must keep focused on the facts. Fact 1: No one can accurately predict the future. Fact 2: Pessimism is a symptoms of depression. Fact 3: With appropriate treatment, four out of five people with even serious depression make a recovery.

If you are self-labeling "I'm a loser . . . I'm a failure . . . I am unlovable," consider these alternatives:

- Self-damning never helps. I've got to be kind and decent to myself (especially during this time of depression).

- Negative labels are inaccurate, gross generalizations. I can't afford to fall prey to this kind of distorted thinking. It's unrealistic, and it makes depression worse.

Here are some useful statements that may also provide support.

- Take one day at a time.

- Whenever possible, take action and avoid passivity or withdrawal.

- Just do it!

- I must treat myself in a compassionate way.

- For now, I can choose to adjust my standards for performance and reevaluate my standards after the depression lifts.

- No matter what others may think, I am trying to do my best.

- To experience frustrations, to suffer disappointments, and to mourn losses are part of the human experience. Often life is hard. That's a fact. I can take some comfort in knowing that fellow human beings have also traveled this road. It's part of the human experience.

- Some life decisions might be best put off until I overcome depression. Not everything has to be done now. I can give myself permission to deal with some issues later.

- It's okay to have limits on what I am able to do just now. It's okay to prioritize. It's okay to say "no."

Chapter Twenty-four

Other Steps to Enhance Self-Esteem and to Nurture Yourself

To further combat low self-esteem try out the following strategies.

Accept compliments. When others offer a compliment, don't reject, minimize, or pooh-pooh it. Say "thanks" and let it sink in. Allow yourself to consider the compliment as an honest and sincere gift. Give yourself permission to consider that the positive comment is true.

Avoid minimizing. Give yourself credit for accomplishments, acts of kindness, or friendship with others. Do not minimize what you do.

Fully examine criticism. When others criticize you, don't automatically take it in as necessarily a statement of truth. If the criticism has some merit, it may be worth considering, but be aware that depressed people are prone to taking criticism to heart without challenging its validity. Often, judgments or criticisms are either inaccurate conclusions on the part of others, or sometimes they are just differences of opinion or perspective. Sometimes they are unwarranted, hurtful barbs designed to put you down or wound you. Consider the source, consider the legitimacy of the remark, and don't automatically assume that you are to blame.

Reframe. Reframe your mistakes. After making a mistake, you can choose to rake yourself over the coals. But a better approach is to:

- Own it. Admit that you did, in fact, make a mistake. Humbly acknowledge that, as a human being, you are not perfect.

- Rather than punish yourself, ask, "What can I learn from this mistake that could help me in the future?"

- Consider that often mistakes are not due solely to personal error.

Many mistakes can be attributed to the following, often overlooked, factors:

- You have no way to really know ahead of time that certain events will unfold as they do (you're not clairvoyant).

- Some choices are made when there truly are no viable alternatives, and yet after the fact, people blame themselves.

- Choices are made under time pressures that may interfere with more careful planning.

- Some situations have no truly good solutions, and people must simply do their best to solve problems. One poignant example may be the choices that are made in the last stages of a terminal illness of a family member; desperate treatments, decisions to remove someone from life support—has anyone truly found the right guidelines for decisions made under those circumstances?

Take good care of yourself. Make an all-out commitment to nurture yourself. Make a list of those life activities that almost always provide some degree of pleasure, joy, or relief. Then give yourself permission to do them—often! Some examples:

- Going to the movies

- Taking a bubble bath

- Buying take-out food rather than cooking

- Taking a day off from work to drive in the country

- Renting a silly video and watching it

- Drinking a root-beer float

- Listening to great music

If you feel any amount of guilt in indulging yourself, then here is a rationalization: it's a requirement. You *must* do these things as a part of your treatment for depression.

Avoid toxic people. Seek out people who are good to you, and stay away from jerks.

Get involved. Pursue hobbies, crafts, volunteer work, continuing education, or sports that you have had some interest in but never done. Stretch yourself, take some risks, and go for it! Reinvent your life, building in more fun and personally meaningful activities.

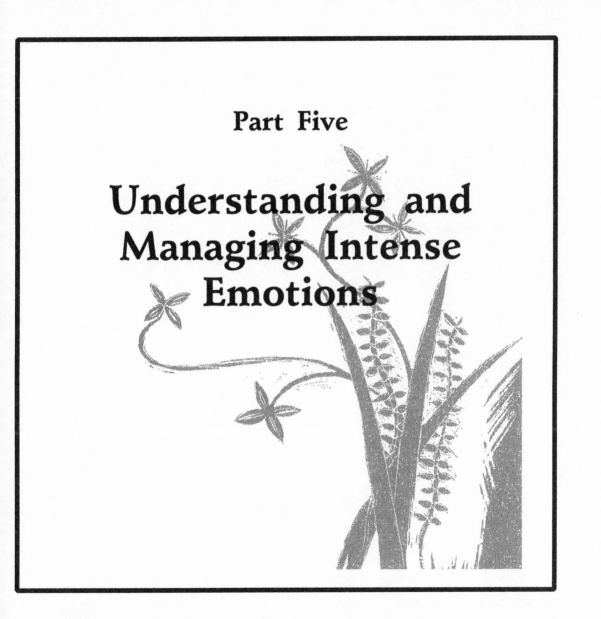

Part Five

Understanding and Managing Intense Emotions

Almost all depressed people experience a noticeable change in emotions. Not only are they confronted by a host of understandable emotions that naturally emerge in response to major life issues (for example, the grief following the loss of a loved one). Additionally, emotions during episodes of depression are often intensified. Many people going through a depression may experience feelings in ways that they have never felt before. Sometimes waves of emotions may seem overwhelming; they may be experienced as exaggerated, inappropriate, or confusing. Eruptions of anger, weeping, or great despair can make you feel totally out of control. And for some people, strong emotions trigger feelings of shame and heightened vulnerability.

In this section of the book we will look at a number of helpful strategies designed to help you understand and more effectively manage strong emotions.

Chapter Twenty-five

Necessary and Unnecessary Emotional Pain

A significant amount of the emotional suffering people encounter when depressed should be seen as not only painful, but also pathological and unhealthy. This type of anguish is the target of treatment for depression. Yet, often buried in among the various elements of emotional distress are certain types of psychological pain that may be deemed natural, healthy, and even necessary.

Noted psychiatrist M. Scott Peck, author of the popular book *The Road Less Traveled* (1978), has described two versions of human emotional suffering: existential pain and neurotic pain. Existential pain is seen as the entirely normal, understandable suffering that all human beings experience in the face of significant losses, frustrations, disappointments, and fears in living. The death of a loved one, receiving a diagnosis of terminal cancer, ongoing racial discrimination, living with chronic pain, abandonment, sexual abuse, domestic violence, the loss of a dream for a happy marriage. None of us are immune to the inevitable emotional pain of such life events. We all have hearts and hearts can be broken. To feel and to express sadness, fear, or anger in response to those very difficult challenges in life is an honest expression of our humanity (a part of human existence—existential).

Dr. Peck goes on to add that it also seems essential, at least to an extent, for people to give in to the experience of these emotions; to allow them into our awareness and to find appropriate outlets for expression (for example, sharing your pain with a trusted friend, relative, or counselor). The expression and sharing of emotions appears to be an essential and necessary ingredient in emotional healing. In fact, many times, suppressed emotions may be a key factor in igniting clinical depression. Yet many people have come to believe:

- I shouldn't burden others.

- I should be strong and keep my feelings under control.

- It never helps to cry.

- To talk about my pain would be just to complain.

Existential pain can be temporarily avoided by gritting your teeth, distracting yourself, or numbing yourself with drugs or alcohol. But those who do best in recovering from depression are those who acknowledge this legitimate, necessary pain and take the difficult path of what psychotherapists call *working through*. Existential pain is not eradicated by antidepressants nor does it simply disappear with the passing of time. Rather, emotional healing can take place as you work through (not "go around" or "get over," but work *through*) your pain by expressing emotions, struggling to find meaning in your suffering, and confiding in others.

But let's be clear; some sources of emotional pain are pathological, unhealthy, and utterly unnecessary. Dr. Peck calls these versions of emotional distress "neurotic pain." Throughout this book, we've spoken about neurotic pain, although not in those particular words. The most common varieties of unnecessary, neurotic pain include: harsh self-criticism, perceptions of the world that are one-sided and skewed in an unrealistically negative way, unrelenting self-blame and shame, "should" statements, and self-hatred.

Your best shot at recovery from depression lies in finding a way to allow the expression of necessary pain. To acknowledge and honor such suffering as legitimate and worthy of compassionate understanding. At the same time, you must be able to recognize those elements of your suffering that emanate from neurotic sources. And such unnecessary pain should then be the target of an all-out assault to defeat the source of this suffering.

During my twenty-five years as a psychotherapist, I have noticed, over and over again, a major turning point in treatment that heralds significant emotional growth and recovery. In one way or another, most depressed people often say, "I shouldn't feel this way. What's wrong with me?" The turning point, I believe, comes as they begin to truly see that certain core aspects of their pain are both legitimate and understandable. I will often hear clients remark, "Of course I've been feeling bad! Just look at what I have had to face in my life (a divorce, loss of a loved one, rejections, betrayal, and so on)." For me, this represents a moment of truth as people see clearly into their hearts, unencumbered by self-judgments and unrealistically critical attitudes. It is often then that healing begins.

Chapter Twenty-six

Open Up and
Gain Control

Psychologist and researcher, Dr. James Pennebaker has conducted extensive studies revealing that pent-up emotions contribute to both physical health problems (such as high blood pressure) and an increased incidence of depression (1990). As you are probably aware, our culture often teaches people, early in life, to keep a lid on emotions. To be emotional is often erroneously equated with immaturity, personal weakness, or hysteria. Yet excessive emotional control can actually interfere with mental health and complicate recovery from depression.

It is interesting to note, however, that most cultures also have rituals designed to promote emotional expression. The best examples are funerals and memorial services. And we have all heard that confession is good for the soul.

When people grit their teeth and try to avoid experiencing or expressing emotions, it frequently leads to a significant increase in rumination and worry. Unexpressed thoughts and emotions have a tendency to persistently spin around in one's mind, eating away at people, and rarely finding resolution. However, when people decide to honestly share inner struggles with a trusted friend, family member, spiritual advisor, or therapist, it is often the first major step toward recovery from depression. Obviously, the critical element in this decision to open up and share is choosing the right person to confide in; someone who can listen, who will not judge, and who will keep confidences.

Pennebaker's breakthrough strategy that can facilitate "opening up" involves what he calls *therapeutic writing*.

- **Step one.** Find a time and place where you will not be disturbed. Have a pen and paper available. And take a moment to relax.

- **Step two.** Begin to write. Write about important, difficult, and painful events that are on your mind. These may also include events that happened a long time ago. What is necessary for this strategy to work is to write about these experiences expressing your *deepest emotions*. This is not like a cut-and-dry newspaper article, but rather a very personal, honest, and emotional exercise.

- **Step three.** Write for about twenty minutes. Really get into it; don't worry about spelling or grammar. No one else will ever read it. Repeat this each day for at least five days in a row.

Remarkably, many people who are otherwise cut off from inner feelings often find therapeutic writing to be a powerful way to access and experience inner, pent-up, or buried emotions.

Pennebaker (in numerous, ingenious studies) has demonstrated that this technique alone can have impressive results. Such outcomes include improved health, decreased blood pressure, an enhanced immune system, and reduced emotional suffering.

Another strategy that Dr. Pennebaker has found is to, rather than writing, speak into a tape recorder for ten or twenty minutes with heartfelt emotions. This technique appears to be especially effective in helping people shut off a busy brain and more easily fall asleep. Some of his research subjects jokingly commented that the tape recorder is kind of like a "psychic vacuum cleaner," which sucks negative thoughts out of their minds.

Like other techniques we've explored in this book, therapeutic writing may seem simplistic. However, do not underestimate the power of this strategy. It's a direct and effective approach that helps people acknowledge and come to terms with inner "necessary pain."

Chapter Twenty-seven

Rapid Solutions for Managing Overwhelming Emotions

During times of depression people may experience moments of extremely intense, painful emotions: anxiety, sadness, despair, anger, and so on. In the previous two chapters we have considered the importance of acknowledging, honoring, and expressing emotional pain (especially "existential," or "necessary pain"). But, let's be honest. Sometimes emotional distress just feels too overpowering. When you are beset by waves of intense emotion, it will be helpful to use effective strategies to manage such feelings in order to reduce suffering and regain some control. This chapter takes a look at four approaches that are often successful in turning the volume down on painful feelings.

Tears of relief. Many people believe that crying is a symptom of depression. Quite possibly, instead of being a symptom, it may be a solution.

Neurobiologist Dr. William Frey has taken the lead in research on crying and the biology of tears (1983). His studies reveal that many people begin to cry, feel ashamed, and then choke back tears. But when people give themselves permission to cry—no shaming, no self-criticism—the experience of crying rapidly reduces a wide range of intense emotions (from sadness to anger). In fact, according to Dr. Frey, 85 percent of women and 73 percent of men report the significant and rapid reduction of painful emotions following an average crying spell, which generally lasts only three to six minutes.

Despite admonitions such as "Don't be a crybaby," "Don't cry over spilled milk," or "Real men don't cry," the truth is that this simple, natural, physical response is *very* effective in reducing intense distress. Why does this work?

I suspect that one reason it helps to cry is that it releases pent-up emotions. Also, it's harder to deny the truth of inner suffering as your eyes fill with tears. However, beyond this, crying appears to directly reduce stress levels. Dr. Frey has shown that nonemotional tears (like those shed due to eye irritation) and emotional tears are significantly different in their chemical makeup. Analysis of the chemical composition of tears reveals that emotional crying is actually eliminating stress hormones from the body, making crying an excretory function.

It is perplexing, unfortunate, and downright stupid that our culture has come to look down on crying. It's natural, it's safe, and it's effective. In fact, if you give yourself permission to cry, in a few minutes you'll likely feel *more* in control! It may seem paradoxical, but it works.

Ten minutes of intense exercise. The rapid increase in serotonin that accompanies intense physical exercise operates to inhibit a wide array of emotions. Do it once and judge for yourself.

The Sixty-Second Reality Check. In part three of this book we learned about a number of techniques designed to improve the clarity and accuracy of your thinking. The Sixty-Second Reality Check (Preston, Varzos and Liebert 2000) is an abbreviated version that can help you quickly gain perspective and rapidly reduce emotional distress. If you're feeling upset. Follow these six instructions:

Sixty-Second Reality Check

1. Ask yourself: What has just happened? What are my feelings and are they understandable?

2. In the grand scheme of things, how important is this?

3. Ask yourself, "Given my strong feelings now, am I likely to be this upset about it twenty-four hours from now? Forty-eight hours from now?"

4. Quickly scan your mind for "shoulds/shouldn'ts," especially: "This shouldn't be happening" and "I shouldn't feel this way." If these are present, say to yourself, "It's not a matter of should or shouldn't. These upsetting events/experiences *are* happening. And I *do* feel bad (sad, irritated, etc.). It's just the truth."

5. If the intense emotion is anxiety or nervousness, do two sets of eye movements (see pages 23–24).

6. Remind yourself: "No matter what, I will not be hard on myself. I must be decent, gentle, and compassionate toward myself."

Okay, maybe it takes ninety seconds, but try it—even once. Most people experience an immediate de-escalation in strong emotions.

Putting it all together. What is most effective is to cry or exercise first, and then do the Sixty-Second Reality Check (thinking generally is more effective and reality based once there is some decrease in emotional arousal).

Riding the waves of emotion. It may seem paradoxical, or hard to believe, but often people are calmed by what is known as *radical acceptance*. Here is how this works: No one likes intensely painful emotions. Yet the path of radical acceptance asks you not to fight the feeling; rather, notice it, acknowledge the truth, "This *is* difficult (or painful)." Then say to yourself, "I don't have to like this, but I can simply accept that this is how I feel in this moment. These are honest human emotions. And, like all emotions, they come in waves. Soon the intensity of this feeling will begin to subside."

The energy expended in fighting off feelings, as odd as it may seem, actually tends to intensify emotions. Once again, I want to encourage you to experiment and give this a try.

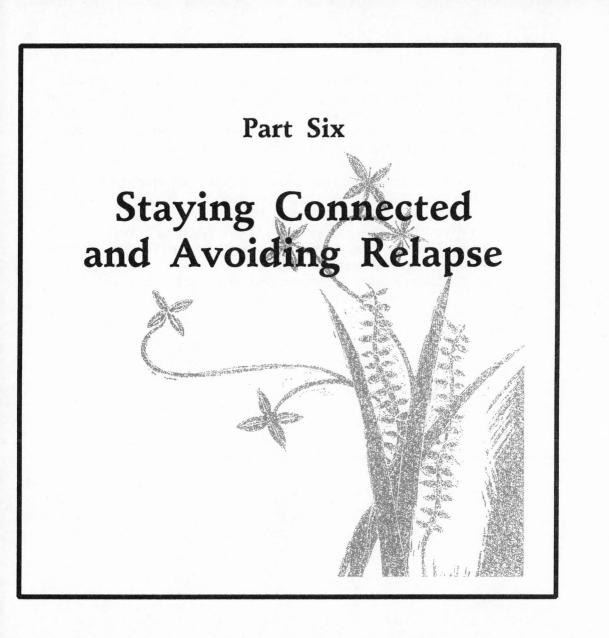

Part Six

Staying Connected
and Avoiding Relapse

A common experience for depressed people is to withdraw. This can include a withdrawal from others, from support, from ordinary life activities, and even from one's own self. When people suffer, it's natural to pull away from others, but the excessive withdrawal seen in depression creates its own set of problems. Just like removing a plant from a source of light, withdrawal can cause a person to wither.

In this part of the book, we will consider strategies aimed at restoring connections with others and also a very important aspect of recovery from depression: uncovering and connecting with your hidden self.

A final approach to staying connected is to stay connected to your life without depression. As we have seen before, depression can recur. Yet there are ways to spot the earliest signs of recurrence and actions to take that can stop it in its tracks. The final chapter looks at recovery and relapse prevention.

Chapter Twenty-eight

Pleasant Activities Therapy

When depression hits, almost without exception, people become more withdrawn. They stay at home, reduce social contacts, and become more sedentary. Many stop answering the phone and even reduce their number of pleasant, at-home activities. A core symptom of depression is a decreased capacity to enjoy life; the sense of vitality evaporates and usual life activities become tedious and boring. Rather than energizing you, even things that ordinarily provide fun and energy end up zapping you and contributing to a generalized sense of despair. In the wake of this phenomenon, no wonder people withdraw.

Withdrawal and social isolation is a symptom of depression, but it's also one of the most significant factors increasing the severity of depression. As the depressed person finds themselves more and more cut off from meaningful and enlivening activities, the more their existence seems barren and drab.

In a number of exceptional studies, Dr. Peter Lewinsohn and colleagues demonstrated that if you encourage (or even force) depressed people to keep socially active, this "treatment" alone can resolve many cases of clinical depression within a few weeks (1984). His approach involves the scheduling of regular social and recreational activities. Then a therapist and family members work together to insist that depressed patients go to these activities. No excuses are accepted; those who agree to participate in Lewinsohn's studies are, in a sense, coerced into staying active, often against their wills! I'm sure you can imagine that many of the people who participated in his research felt tired, unmotivated, and completely nonenthusiastic, as they were pushed out the front door headed for movies, square dancing, bowling, or other agreed-upon activities. Of course, in the first couple of weeks there were complaints and moaning. But the remarkable outcome was that this "forced fun" started to make a real difference.

This approach is tough, if not impossible to do alone; it's important (maybe essential) for you to get a buddy or coach (perhaps a family member or good friend) to provide encouragement.

Step one. Consult appendix C for a list of various activities (these are activities that have been judged to be pleasant by many people), and place a check mark next to those that you're willing to do.

Step two. Get a calendar and schedule activities *every day* for the next week. At first, this may seem like overkill, but the intent is to stay active and engaged (some of these activities are more involved while some are as simple as taking a walk around the block or watching the sunset).

Step three. Speak openly with your "coach," telling them that you want their help in making sure you follow through with scheduled activities. This might, at times, require them to accompany you. At other times, it may be done by simply calling the friend from the zoo, movie theater, etc., and telling them, "I made it. Thanks for your help."

Step four. Use the Satisfaction Prediction Sheet (see page 68) to help you keep motivated. And, regardless of the amount of enjoyment, continue for a month. Recall that early in treatment, most participants in Lewinsohn's study did not fully enjoy activities, but that a shift in enjoyment did begin to occur in a week or two.

Chapter Twenty-nine

To Thine Own Self Be True: Staying Connected to You

Joann was perplexed. Why had she become so depressed during the past six months? As she took stock of her life, it seemed clear that nothing really bad had happened; no losses, no tragedies, absolutely nothing that might explain her low mood. So she felt uncomfortable and somewhat confused as she went in for her first session with a therapist.

"I have a good life . . . good kids, good husband . . . financially we are secure. I don't have any reason to be depressed." Her therapist listened carefully and then encouraged Joann to just talk a bit about herself, taking her time to look closely at her life.

During the first three sessions, as Joann shared her thoughts about her life with her therapist, a theme began to emerge. In so many ways, she had devoted her life to caring for the needs of others. For instance, as a dutiful daughter in high school, she was quick to put her own needs aside for the sake of her younger brother or to make life easier for her parents. Likewise, in her married life, she had settled into a role in which she was always there for everyone; to fix things, to listen, to rescue, to console. What started to become increasingly clear was that somewhere along the path of her life, she had set aside her inner self (her needs, her feelings, even her own beliefs) to take care of others. And this had been done to excess. Joann had lost touch with her inner self.

Life roles that are totally devoted to caring for others, those based on excessive compliance, a strong desire to never make waves, or to live out the dreams of others (like making career choices favored by a parent) can and do often leave people estranged from their own inner self. And, often this can set the stage for depression. Most times such depressions come on gradually. And like Joann, the source of the depression is often at first, an ill-defined mystery.

One of the most important sources of vitality, enjoyment, and aliveness comes from living a life that is in synch with who you really are. A life burdened by overcompliance or excessive sacrifice of the self can choke off aliveness just as sure as moving a plant out of the light can cause it to wither.

Confiding in another (for example, a therapist or trusted friend) can often lead one to greater clarity about inner, but suppressed, needs, urges, and feelings. Therapeutic writing also may lead one to a greater awareness of a buried, inner self (see page 116). Additionally, you may find the following exercise helpful. Take a few minutes, read the questions, reflect, and write down your thoughts.

Part one: My role in life, as scripted by others

1. What are/were my parents' dreams or goals for me in terms of life style, career, and relationships? How did they really want me to "turn out"?

2. In what ways have I not fulfilled my parents' hopes or dreams?

3. What are two or three times during childhood or adolescence where I can recall having a significant difference of opinion with my parents. Then reflect: looking back on this now, what might this tell me about myself (my personal or unique beliefs, values, desires, or needs)?

4. In what ways have I inhibited myself (not followed my own desires or instincts) in order to either please my parents (or others) or to avoid their criticism?

5. In present-day relationships (as a husband, wife, as a parent, as a friend, as an employee) what do others want or expect from me? What roles do they want me to play?

6. How am I currently inhibiting myself?

7. What roles or expectations, imposed on me by others, do I know, in my heart of hearts, are not my choosing? What roles or expectations do I privately resent or feel burdened by?

Part two: My life on my terms

1. Setting aside all pressures to conform or meet others' needs, at least for a few minutes in my mind, what would I most like to do (social activities, recreation, career, education, relationships, qualities I'd like

in intimate relationships, daily schedules, living arrangements, household chores, where I'd like to live, and so on). Explore this thoroughly—really get into this exercise! Using your wildest imagination, write a script (as if you were creating a character for a novel) for a life/lifestyle based entirely on your inner needs, desires, values, and talents.

2. After completing the script, sit with this a bit, reflect, and then honestly ask yourself, "To what degree am I living my life in accord with my unique inner self?" Such an exercise can often help one identify chronic sources of dissatisfaction or disappointment that may be spurring depression, and which may also point to possible solutions.

It is common for most people to be only vaguely aware of such inner disappointments or the underlying loss of self. Self-discovery can be an important step in addressing problems that you may be having in relationships or in your current lifestyle. But be prepared, because this kind of examination can also result in a painful awakening. Honestly confronting inner truths is often a key ingredient in successful recovery from depression. Often, what is equally important is to then take actions to change your life. This may involve more open discussions with intimate others, requesting and negotiating for changes in relationships, or deciding upon new directions in your educational or career pursuits.

The best shot we humans have at creating a life worth living may rest, in part, in being able to discover who we truly are, and then living life in accord with our own inner needs, desires, values, and beliefs.

Chapter Thirty

Recovery and Relapse Prevention

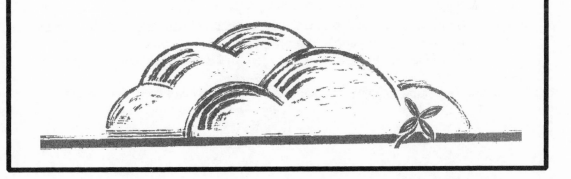

Almost everyone who makes a recovery from depression will encounter brief set-backs. The road to recovery is not a straight path.

It's very important to keep clear about this and avoid a common tendency to conclude that "the depression is back" when, for instance, you experience a day or two in which you feel more depressed. Hang in there—most times the return of depressive symptoms is temporary.

About one half of people who experience depression will encounter it again at some point in their lifetime. But the good news is that if you can recognize the early signs of a recurrence and take immediate action, most of the time it can be nipped in the bud and another episode can be averted. Your best shot at spotting the early signs of recurring depression lies in being alert to early, subtle signs. These can vary a lot from person to person. If you can recall the first symptoms of depression you experienced in this current episode, they may very well be the first ones to appear again, should you have a recurrence. Research has demonstrated that for most people the early warning sign that comes on the scene first is problems with sleep. So be especially alert to this.

Denial or the decision to "tough it out" should symptoms reappear is common, but it simply does not make sense. Stay alert, be honest with yourself, use sound judgment, and if necessary, do not hesitate to take action should you sense that depression is beginning to emerge.

Finally, it's worth repeating: the nature of depression is that it results in extreme pessimism. This is manifest in a number of ways, and most of the time it is evident in the strongly held belief, "I'll never get over this depression." For the vast majority of depressed people, the prognosis is very good and with appropriate action (self-help and professional treatment) it is *very* likely that you can overcome this.

I sincerely hope that you have found this book to be of help. Best wishes.

Appendix A

Check Out Your
Biology

Depression can be, and often is, a reaction to stressful live events. However, it's important to note that it can also be due to a number of conditions that affect brain chemistry. Before embarking on psychotherapy, antidepressant medication treatment, or self-help, it is crucial to make sure that depressive symptoms are not due to some kind of medical problem.

Physical/Medical Exam

Not everyone suffering from depression needs a physical/medical exam. However, if any of the following apply to you, a visit to your primary-care doctor is an important first step.

- Depression has emerged, but there are *no* identifiable recent life stresses.

- The current depressive symptoms have never occurred before (it's your first episode of depression), and you are over forty-five years old.

- There are significant physical symptoms, such as pain, changes in vision, marked fatigue, substantial weight gain or weight loss.

A physical exam and laboratory tests generally are able to diagnose or rule out most medical causes of depression. In most cases, when primary medical disorders are treated, depressive symptoms will subside. At times, treatment for depression may also be necessary. Listed below are common diseases and disorders that may cause depression (Preston, O'Neal, Talaga 2000).

Medical Disorders That Can Cause Depression

- Addison's disease
- AIDS
- Anemia
- Asthma
- Chronic fatigue syndrome
- Chronic infection (mononucleosis, tuberculosis)
- Chronic pain
- Congestive heart failure
- Cushing's disease
- Diabetes
- Hyperthyroidsim
- Hypothyroidism

- Infectious hepatitis
- Influenza
- Malignancies (cancer)
- Malnutrition
- Multiple sclerosis
- Parkinson's disease
- Porphyria
- Rheumatoid arthritis
- Sleep apnea
- Syphilis
- Sytemic lupus erythematosus
- Ulcerative colitis
- Uremia

Medications, Substance Use and Abuse

Many prescription drugs can cause depression in some individuals. Again, it's important to know if medications are the culprit. Common medications that can cause depression are listed below (Preston, O'Neal, Talaga 2000).

Drugs That Can Cause Depression

Type	Generic name	Brand name
Alcohol	Wine, beer, spirits	Various brands
Antianxiety drugs	Diazepam	Valium
	Chlordiazepoxide	Librium
	Lorazepam	Ativam
	Alprazolam	Xanax
Antihypertensives (for high blood pressure or migraine headache)	Reserpine	Serpasil, Ser-Ap-Es
	Propranolol hydrochloride	Inderal
	Methyldopa	Aldomet
	Guanethidine sulfate	Ismelin sulfate
	Clonidine hydrochloride	Catapres
	Hydralazine hydrochloride	Apresoline hydrochloride
Antiparkinsonian drugs	Levodopa carbidopa	Sinemet
	Levodopa	Dupar, Larodopa
	Amantadine hydrochloride	Symmetrel
Birth control pills	Progestin-estrogen combination	Various brands
Corticosteroids and other hormones	Cortisone acetate	Cortone
	Estrogen	Premarin, Ogen, Estrace, Estraderm
	Progesterone and derivatives	Provera, Depo-Provera, Norlutate, Norplant, Progestasert

Additionally, legal and illicit recreational drugs *often* cause depression. Those most likely to do so include:

- Stimulants: amphetamines and cocaine (after long-term use)
- Marijuana (heavy use)
- Alcohol (wine, beer, spirits)

Hormonal Changes

A number of hormonal changes can cause significant alterations in mood. The most common are thyroid abnormalities and fluctuating levels of female sex hormones (especially noticeable around reproductive events, such as the premenstrual period, following childbirth, and at menopause). Make sure these are evaluated when getting a physical exam.

Severe Disruption of Sleep Cycles

Frequent changes in work schedules among those who are shift workers may disturb the circadian rhythm and sleep patterns. For some, this can result in depression. Another not-infrequent cause of depression (but a disorder that is often not recognized) is sleep apnea. Apnea is a sleep disorder characterized by abnormal respiration during sleep. If you have realized or have been told by others that you snore, it's a red flag for possible apnea. Many people have suffered for years with fatigue and depression to finally be diagnosed with apnea. This sleep disorder is often very successfully treated.

Appendix B

Stay Connected: Web Sites and Support Groups

If you cruise the information highway, you might check out the following Web sites:

National Mental Health Association
1021 Prince Street
Alexandria, VA. 22314
(800) 969-6642
www.nmha.org
nmhainfo@aol.com

Depression Awareness, Recognition, Treatment; National Institute
    of Mental Health
5600 Fishers Lane
Rockville, MD 20857
(800) 421-4211
www.nimh.nih.gov/newdart
Publications in Spanish, Russian, Asian

National Foundation for Depressive Illness, Inc.
P.O. Box 2257
New York, NY 10116
(800) 239-1265
www.depression.org

National Depressive and Manic-Depressive Association
730 N. Franklin Street, Suite 501
Chicago, IL 60610
(800) 826-3632
www.ndmda.org
myrtis@aol.com

John Preston
www.Psyd-fx.com

Also, check with these organizations or your local Mental Health Association to find out about depression support groups.

Appendix C

Pleasant Activities

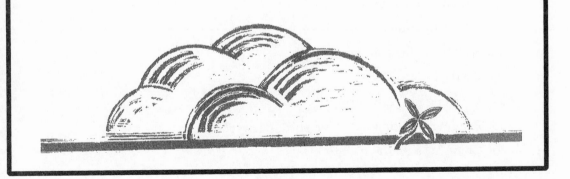

The best activities to choose are those you have enjoyed in the past. However, when people are depressed, it's often hard to think of even one potentially pleasant activity. Listed below are some suggestions to get you started. It will also be a good idea to sit down with a close friend or family member and with their help, brainstorm. Come up with a list of activities you've done in the past and others that you have never considered. In addition to enjoyable activities also consider things you can do that would be interesting or meaningful.

1. Reading novels or magazines

2. Watching TV

3. Renting and watching a video

4. Learn a new craft or hobby (many craft stores offer classes)

5. Camping

6. Working in politics or for a political or social cause

7. Having lunch with friends

8. Taking a shower

9. Being with animals

10. Singing in a group

11. Going to church socials

12. Playing a musical instrument

13. Going to the beach

14. Rearranging your furniture

15. Reading the Bible or other spiritual works

16. Going to a sports event

17. Playing sports
18. Going to the movies
19. Cooking meals
20. Having a good cry
21. Going to a restaurant
22. Looking at beautiful flowers or plants
23. Saying prayers
24. Canning, making preserves, etc.
25. Taking a bath
26. Making food or crafts to sell or give away
27. Painting or drawing
28. Visiting people who are sick or shut in
29. Bowling
30. Gardening or doing yard work
31. Shopping
32. Sitting in the sun
33. Going to a zoo or amusement park
34. Playing board games
35. Doing outdoor work
36. Reading the newspaper
37. Swimming

38. Running, jogging, or walking

39. While taking a walk, try to see new things you have never noticed before

40. Playing Frisbee

41. Listening to music

42. Knitting, crocheting, or needlework

43. Starting a new project

44. Having sex

45. Bird watching

46. Repairing things

47. Bicycling

48. Giving gifts

49. Going on outings (to the park or a picnic)

50. Playing basketball

51. Helping someone

52. Seeing beautiful scenery

53. Hiking

54. Going to a museum

55. Fishing

56. Going to a health club

57. Writing letters, cards, or notes

58. Going to luncheons, potlucks, etc.

59. Being with my husband or wife

60. Going on field trips, nature walks, etc.

61. Expressing my love to someone

62. Caring for houseplants

63. Collecting things

64. Sewing

65. Going to auctions, garage sales, etc.

66. Doing volunteer work

67. Seeing old friends

68. Writing to old friends

69. Calling old friends

70. Going to the library

Recommended
Readings

Beck, A. T. 1976. *Cognitive Therapy and the Emotional Disorders* New York: New American Library.

Bender, K. J. 1998. Dietary fatty acids essential for mental health. *Psychiatric Times*, December, 1998, p. 22-24.

Byrne, A., and D. G. Byrne. 1993. The effect of exercise on depression, anxiety and other mood states: a review. *Journal of Psychosomatic Research* (376):565-574.

Dahlitz, M., B. Alvarez, J. Vignau, et al. 1991. Delayed sleep phase syndrome response to melatonin. *The Lancet* 337:1121-1125.

Dement, W. C., and M. M. Mitler. 1993. It's time to wake up to the importance of sleep disorders. *JAMA* 269:1548-1551.

Dey, S. 1994. Physical exercise as a novel antidepressant agent: possible role of serotonin receptor subtypes. *Physiological Behavior* 55(2):323-29.

Fernstrom, J. D. 1994. Dietary amino acids and brain function. *Journal of the American Dietetic Association* 94:71-77.

Hobson, A. J. 1995. *Sleep.* New York: Scientific American Library.

Jarrett, D. B. 1989. Chronobiology. In *Comprehensive Textbook of Psychiatry*: Fifth Edition. Edited by Kaplan and Sadock. Baltimore: Williams and Wilkins.

Kagan, B. 1990. Oral SAM-e in depression. *Archives of General Psychiatry* 147: 591-595.

Klerman, G. L., and M. M. Weissman. 1984. *Interpersonal Psychotherapy of Depression.* New York: Basic Books.

Lewy, A. J. 1996. The use of light and melatonin to change circadian rhythms. *Audio Digest Psychiatry* 25(23). Glendale, CA: Audio Digest Foundation.

Preston, J. D. 2001. *You Can Beat Depression.* San Luis Obispo, CA: Impact Publishers.

Preston J. D., J. H. O'Neal, and M. T. Talaga. 2001. *Handbook of Clinical Psychopharmacology for Therapists*. Oakland: New Harbinger Publications.

Raglin, J. S. 1990. Exercise and mental health. *Sports Medicine* 9(6):323-29.

Raskin, V. D. 1997. *When Words Are Not Enough: The Woman's Prescription for Depression and Anxiety*. New York: Broadway Books.

Wurtman, R., and J. Wurtman. 1989. Carbohydrates and depression. *Scientific American*, January, 68-75.

References

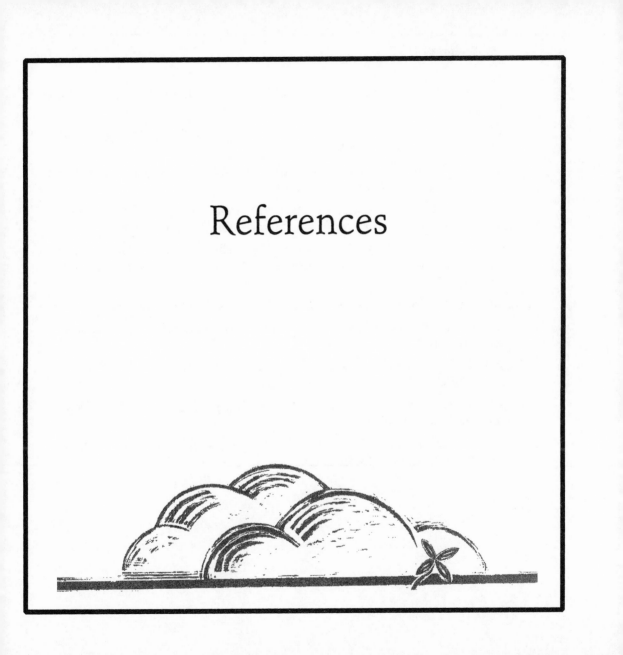

Burns, D. D. 1999. *The Feeling Good Handbook*. Revised Edition. New York: Plume Books.

Frey, W. H., and C. Hoffman-Ahern. 1983. Crying behavior in the human adult. *Integrative Psychiatry* 1:94–100.

Leith, L. M. 1998. *Exercise Your Way to Better Mental Health*. Morgantown, WV: Fitness Information Technology, Inc.

Lewinsohn, P. M. 1984. *The Coping with Depression Course: A Psychoeducational Intervention for Unipolar Depression*. Eugene, OR: Castalia Press.

MacPhillamy, D., and P. M. Lewinsohn. 1982. The pleasant events schedule: Studies in reliability, validity, and scale. *Journal of Consulting and Clinical Psychology* 50:363-380.

Peck, M. S. 1978. *The Road Less Traveled*. New York: Simon and Schuster.

Pennebaker, J. W. 1990. *Opening Up: The Healing Power of Confiding in Others*. New York: Morrow.

Preston, J. D., J. H. O'Neal, and M. C. Talaga. 2000. *Consumer's Guide to Psychiatric Drugs*. Oakland: New Harbinger Publications.

———. 2001. *Handbook of Clinical Psychopharmacology for Therapists*. 2d ed. Okland: New Harbinger Publications.

Preston, J. D., N. Varzos, and D. S. Liebert. 2000. *Make Every Session Count*. Oakland: New Harbinger Publications.

John Preston, Psy.D., is a clinical psychologist and the author of ten books. He is on the faculty of the University of California, Davis School of Medicine and, Alliant University, Sacramento. He has lectured widely in the United States and abroad. He is the recipient of the Mental Health Association's President's Award for contributions to the mental health profession.

Some Other New Harbinger Self-Help Titles

Juicy Tomatoes, $13.95
Help for Hairpullers, $13.95
The Anxiety & Phobia Workbook, Third Edition, $19.95
Thinking Pregnant, $13.95
Rosacea, $13.95
Shy Bladder Syndrome, $13.95
The Adoption Reunion Survival Guide, $13.95
The Queer Parent's Primer, $14.95
Children of the Self-Absorbed, $14.95
Beyond Anxiety & Phobia, $19.95
The Money Mystique, $13.95
Toxic Coworkers, $13.95
The Conscious Bride, $12.95
The Family Recovery Guide, $15.95
The Assertiveness Workbook, $14.95
Write Your Own Prescription for Stress, $13.95
The Shyness and Social Anxiety Workbook, $15.95
The Anger Control Workbook, $17.95
Family Guide to Emotional Wellness, $24.95
Undefended Love, $13.95
The Great Big Book of Hope, $15.95
Don't Leave it to Chance, $13.95
Emotional Claustrophobia, $12.95
The Relaxation & Stress Reduction Workbook, Fifth Edition, $19.95
The Loneliness Workbook, $14.95
Thriving with Your Autoimmune Disorder, $16.95
Illness and the Art of Creative Self-Expression, $13.95
The Interstitial Cystitis Survival Guide, $14.95
Outbreak Alert, $15.95
Don't Let Your Mind Stunt Your Growth, $10.95
Energy Tapping, $14.95
Under Her Wing, $13.95
Self-Esteem, Third Edition, $15.95
Women's Sexualitites, $15.95
Knee Pain, $14.95
Helping Your Anxious Child, $12.95
Breaking the Bonds of Irritable Bowel Syndrome, $14.95
Multiple Chemical Sensitivity: A Survival Guide, $16.95
Dancing Naked, $14.95
Why Are We Still Fighting, $15.95
From Sabotage to Success, $14.95
Parkinson's Disease and the Art of Moving, $15.95
A Survivor's Guide to Breast Cancer, $13.95
Men, Women, and Prostate Cancer, $15.95
Make Every Session Count: Getting the Most Out of Your Brief Therapy, $10.95
Virtual Addiction, $12.95
After the Breakup, $13.95
Why Can't I Be the Parent I Want to Be?, $12.95
The Secret Message of Shame, $13.95
The OCD Workbook, $18.95
Tapping Your Inner Strength, $13.95
Binge No More, $14.95

Call **toll free, 1-800-748-6273,** or log on to our online bookstore at **www.newharbinger.com** to order. Have your Visa or Mastercard number ready. Or send a check for the titles you want to New Harbinger Publications, Inc., 5674 Shattuck Ave., Oakland, CA 94609. Include $4.50 for the first book and 75¢ for each additional book, to cover shipping and handling. (California residents please include appropriate sales tax.) Allow two to five weeks for delivery.

Prices subject to change without notice.